D0563923

GIRAFFE
EXTINCTION

· ·

USING **SCIENCE** AND **TECHNOLOGY**
TO SAVE THE **GENTLE GIANTS**

TANYA ANDERSON

TWENTY-FIRST CENTURY BOOKS / MINNEAPOLIS

Twenty-First Century Books™
An imprint of Lerner Publishing Group, Inc.
241 First Avenue North
Minneapolis, MN 55401 USA

For reading levels and more information, look up this title at www.lernerbooks.com.

Main body text set in Adobe Garamond Pro.
Typeface provided by Adobe Systems.

Library of Congress Cataloging-in-Publication Data

Names: Anderson, Tanya, author.
Title: Giraffe extinction : using science and technology to save the gentle giants / Tanya
   Anderson.
Description: Minneapolis : Twenty-First Century Books, [2020] | Audience: Age
   13–19. | Audience: Grade 9 to 12. | Includes bibliographical references and index. |
Identifiers: LCCN 2018054714 (print) | LCCN 2018056497 (ebook) |
   ISBN 9781541562660 (eb pdf) | ISBN 9781541532380 (lb : alk. paper)
Subjects: LCSH: Giraffe—Conservation—Juvenile literature. | Endangered species—
   Conservation—Juvenile literature.
Classification: LCC QL737.U56 (ebook) | LCC QL737.U56 A55 2020 (print) | DDC
   599.638—dc23

LC record available at https://lccn.loc.gov/2018054714

Manufactured in the United States of America
1-44839-35710-3/26/2019

CONTENTS

CHAPTER 1
DISAPPEARING SHADOWS   4

CHAPTER 2
TRACKING DOWN THE NUMBERS   20

CHAPTER 3
SCIENCE HAS SOME SURPRISES   32

CHAPTER 4
HABITAT LOSS AND FRAGMENTATION   48

CHAPTER 5
HUMAN VIOLENCE AND CLIMATE CHANGE   60

CHAPTER 6
THE GOOD NEWS OF GIRAFFE CONSERVATION   78

CHAPTER 7
SPEAKING UP FOR GIRAFFES   94

GIRAFFE GUIDE   101
GLOSSARY   111
SOURCE NOTES   114
SELECTED BIBLIOGRAPHY   117
FURTHER INFORMATION   122
INDEX   125

CHAPTER 1
DISAPPEARING SHADOWS

- -

I HAD TIME AFTER TIME WATCHED THE
PROGRESSION ACROSS THE PLAIN OF THE
GIRAFFE, IN THEIR QUEER, INIMITABLE, VEGETATIVE
GRACEFULNESS AS IF IT WERE NOT A HERD
OF ANIMALS BUT A FAMILY OF RARE, LONG-
STEMMED, SPECKLED, GIGANTIC FLOWERS SLOWLY
ADVANCING. IT WAS IN GIANT SIZE, THE BORDER
OF A VERY OLD, INFINITELY PRECIOUS PERSIAN
CARPET IN THE DYES OF GREEN, YELLOW, AND
BLACK-BROWN.

—ISAK DINESEN, *OUT OF AFRICA*

- -

Danish writer Isak Dinesen had the privilege of watching giraffes in their native African landscapes. She and others who have shared the same pleasure say the experience moved and even changed them. No other creatures on Earth can compare to these gentle giants. Their unusual beauty and mysterious behaviors have captured the imaginations of people for thousands

Giraffes are native to the grassy plains of Africa south of the Sahara. This tower (group) of reticulated giraffes are at the Ewaso Nyiro River in the Samburu National Reserve in Kenya.

of years. More than ten thousand years ago, ancient tribespeople of the African continent etched into giant rock images of thin, long-necked animals covered in spots. Later, Egyptian pharaohs and then Roman rulers included live giraffes in elaborate triumphal parades. Rulers of ancient Middle Eastern empires offered live giraffes as gifts to leaders they wanted to impress, sending the delicate giants as far away as China and Europe.

In more modern times, big-game hunters tracked down giraffes as one of the most coveted trophy animals. In the late nineteenth century, giraffes were hunted almost to extinction. By 1906 giraffes were some of the rarest of species in South Africa.

Giraffes remain an iconic symbol of Africa's rich and varied wildlife. Zoos around the world have always included giraffes in their

Giraffe petroglyphs cover rock surfaces at the Twyfelfontein site in northwestern Namibia. The site has one of the largest numbers of petroglyphs in Africa. In 2007 the United Nations Educational, Scientific and Cultural Organization (UNESCO) approved it as a World Heritage Site.

popular menageries. Visitors love to get a real-life look at the world's tallest animal. Giraffes may have become familiar wildlife to most people, but they have never lost their mystique or their ability to impress anyone who takes a good look into their big, dark eyes.

Most of us assumed giraffes would always be with us. We saw their images in magazines, in film footage of documentaries about Africa, as a part of logos for children's toys, and in colorful illustrations in coloring books and children's literature. So reports that the survival of giraffes in the wild is threatened, coming from experts who have been working with giraffes over the last several years, came as a shock.

The survival of giraffes is critical because the giraffe is a keystone species and ranks among the megafauna, or large animals, on the savannas, or grassy plains, of Africa. A keystone species is one upon which other species in an ecosystem largely depend. If that species were

> "THESE GENTLE GIANTS HAVE BEEN OVERLOOKED. IT'S WELL KNOWN THAT AFRICAN ELEPHANTS ARE IN TROUBLE, AND THERE ARE PERHAPS JUST UNDER HALF A MILLION LEFT. BUT WHAT NO ONE HAS [REALIZED] IS THERE ARE FAR FEWER GIRAFFES, WHICH HAVE ALREADY BECOME EXTINCT IN SEVEN COUNTRIES."
>
> —DAVID ATTENBOROUGH, BRITISH NATURALIST, 2016

to disappear, the ecosystem would change drastically. Giraffes eat the leaves and twigs from near the top of acacia trees, and as the animals forage for food, they naturally prune the trees. Giraffes inadvertently eat the seeds from these trees too. Giraffe dung deposits the seeds on the ground where new trees can then grow. Without giraffes, the savannas would have far fewer acacia trees. The landscape and other wildlife that depend on the trees would lose an important source of food, shade, and nesting material.

The Namibia-based Giraffe Conservation Foundation describes the growing giraffe crisis as a "silent extinction." The foundation and other conservation organizations and giraffe experts have been following and watching these animals and documenting and analyzing data about them. Their conclusions are cause for alarm. Within just thirty years, from 1985 to 2015, the overall population of giraffes in the wild plummeted by 40 percent. In 1985 between 150,000 and 163,000 giraffes roamed the African savannas. By 2015 fewer than 98,000 giraffes existed in the wild. Giraffes have become extinct in at least seven countries where they once made their home.

WHAT HAPPENED?

Wildlife conservation is important for the survival of species all over the planet. The International Union for Conservation of Nature (IUCN), based in Gland, Switzerland, is one of many watchdogs that keeps an eye on and ranks the survival status of Earth's plant and animal species. The organization keeps track of which species are of least concern, which have become extinct, and which are in categories in between. When we hear that the western lowland gorilla *(Gorilla gorilla)* is critically endangered, it's because the IUCN Red List of Threatened Species has gathered data about the animal and ranked it according to the animal's overall population and the threats it faces. The blue whale, the ivory-billed woodpecker, and the red panda are in serious decline too. So far, the IUCN has assessed more than ninety thousand species for inclusion on the Red List. More than twenty-five thousand of those plant and animal species are threatened with extinction. IUCN director general Inger Andersen says, "Many species are slipping away before we can even describe them."

WHAT IS THE IUCN?

The International Union for Conservation of Nature defines itself as "the global authority on the status of the natural world and the measures needed to safeguard it." The IUCN's Red List of Threatened Species is the world's most comprehensive list of the conservation status of plant and animal species. Scientists have evaluated more than ninety thousand species for the list. Of those species, more than twenty-five thousand are considered threatened with extinction. Reports on its website offer detailed information from research experts about threats, ecological issues, and habitats, as well as conservation actions that must be pursued to protect a species from extinction.

HOW IS THE RED LIST USED?

Scientists, researchers, environmental leaders, conservation organizations, and others use the list to evaluate the information on the list as they watch for key trends. Is an animal's population increasing, decreasing, or remaining stable? Is the territory where that species lives growing smaller? Are females reproducing at levels that guarantee

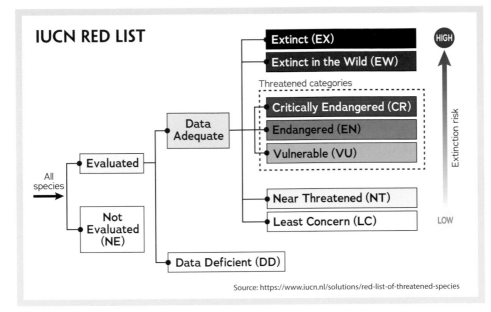

IUCN RED LIST

Extinct (EX)

Extinct in the Wild (EW)

Threatened categories

Critically Endangered (CR)

Endangered (EN)

Vulnerable (VU)

Near Threatened (NT)

Least Concern (LC)

Data Adequate

Evaluated

All species

Not Evaluated (NE)

Data Deficient (DD)

HIGH

Extinction risk

LOW

Source: https://www.iucn.nl/solutions/red-list-of-threatened-species

This infographic shows the IUCN rankings of species that are of Least Concern (at low risk of extinction) to those that are Extinct. The chart also reflects the availability of data for determining rankings.

continuation of the species? How many juveniles of a species are living to adulthood?

On the international stage, nations develop agreements about environmental issues. For example, national environmental leaders will review IUCN data about a species' status to determine whether to allow the hunting of that animal. If the data shows the animal's population and reproduction are strong, nations in which the animal lives are likely to allow hunting. If the data shows the opposite, those nations are more likely to restrict or ban hunting.

Researchers use the data from the most current list to write academic reports and papers for others to consult in their studies and agreements. Conservation groups rely on the data to establish action plans to support the animals or plants they are working to protect. The list also indicates which ecosystems are impacted by the loss of certain species. For example, consider the loss of bees in our world.

Bees are one of nature's key pollinators. More than half of the world's flowering plants and 80 percent of all food crops depend on bees for reproduction. But the number of bees is on the decline because of habitat loss, pesticides, and other factors. So the ecosystems and croplands in which they live face reduced levels of pollination and lower crop yields. This domino effect of loss affects other species, including human beings.

The list also offers good news. It reports improvements in the conditions and numbers of once nearly extinct creatures. In 2017, for example, the IUCN Red List was able to adjust the status of the black-footed ferret *(Mustela nigripes)* of the southwestern United States and northern Mexico. At one time, the ferret was listed as extinct in the wild. Thanks to successful conservation efforts, the ferret is no longer extinct, though it is still endangered. It's a move in the right direction. The humpback whale got a better report card too. In 2008 the IUCN upgraded that whale's status from Threatened to Least Concern.

HOW OFTEN IS THE RED LIST UPDATED?

Conservationists and other scientists use IUCN data in their work. They also provide ongoing data to the IUCN about species worldwide. This information includes updated population counts, changes in a species' taxonomy (scientific classification), the species' geographic distribution, and other critical data. To ensure the newest and most reliable information is available for researchers, the IUCN updates the Red List at least twice each year.

GIRAFFES AND THE IUCN RED LIST

Until recently, the IUCN Red List status for giraffes had been Least Concern. Scientists and researchers had taken giraffe well-being for granted and had never assessed the animal's population data. So no one knew of any reason for alarm. Data collected in 1985 showed the combined populations of all giraffe subspecies to be healthy at about 160,000 animals. But in 2015, the IUCN Red List report came out, showing a 40 percent decline in the number of giraffes in the wild. The status for the giraffe species *Giraffa camelopardalis* immediately jumped two categories, from Least Concern to Vulnerable—and the news went viral.

Julian Fennessy, cofounder of the Nairobi-based Giraffe Conservation Foundation and cochair of the IUCN's Giraffe and Okapi Specialist Group, says, "[While giraffes] are commonly seen on safari, in the media and in zoos, people—including conservationists—are unaware that these majestic animals are undergoing a silent extinction. With a decline of almost 40% in the last three decades alone, the world's tallest animal is under severe pressure in some of its core ranges across East, Central and West Africa. As one of the world's most iconic animals, it is timely that we stick our necks out for giraffe before it is too late."

A WOMAN'S WORK IN AFRICA

Somehow the giraffe's slow march toward extinction had been overlooked. How could that be when this species is literally head, neck, and shoulders above the rest? How could we not know that these elegant, towering creatures were fading from the scene?

The answer is complicated. Until very recently, not much was known about the giraffe. Scientists had assumed a lot of "facts" about the species. For example, most biologists thought the giraffe was mute. (It isn't.) Biologists also believed that the giraffe's long neck is an evolutionary design that came about to help the animals reach leaves on tall branches for eating. (Other theories have since developed.) And the scientific world had treated the giraffe as one species. (New technology challenges this assumption.)

For centuries, the scientific world focused mainly on categorizing animals, not understanding them. Then, in the 1950s, a young Canadian woman stepped onto a continent unfamiliar to her, with one goal: to learn all she could about nature's tallest animal. Anne Innis was born in Toronto, Ontario, Canada. In the 1930s, when she was two years old, she and her family visited Brookfield Zoo, near Chicago, Illinois. There, she remembers seeing her first giraffe.

"Perhaps their height, especially from a small child's perspective, impressed me; perhaps it was the rush of movement when something startled them and they cantered in a flurry of long necks and legs across their paddock. Whatever it was, the giraffe immediately became my [favorite] animal," she recalls in her autobiography, *Pursuing Giraffe.* She didn't see another giraffe for fifteen years, when she and her mother returned to Brookfield Zoo. She says, "My passion for [the] giraffe was firmer than ever."

Innis seemed destined to spend her life studying giraffes. She studied biology at the University of Toronto. Her courses were a solid base for her later work, but it taught her little about animal behavior and even less about African animals. Undeterred, she decided to continue her education, working for a master's degree in genetics. Still, she was determined to study giraffes in the wild. As unremarkable as that might sound today, at the time, she was asking the near impossible. She says,

> In the 1950s, . . . there was no tradition of zoology students or professors doing field research overseas, and, of course, no money or infrastructure for this. Indeed, I was apparently the first zoologist to go to Africa to carry out a long-term scientific study on the [behavior] of a wild mammal.
>
> I would be followed by men studying [different mammals], and, four years later, by Jane Goodall observing chimpanzees. . . . However, back then if I did mention my ambition to study giraffe in Africa to faculty members or anyone else, they laughed heartily at its absurdity.

To study giraffes in the wild meant finding someone in Africa who would be willing to host her for a few months. She knew no one in Africa, so she wrote letter after letter to government officials and wildlife organizations in African nations where giraffes were known to live. She received little encouragement and even some rebuffs from some of the correspondents. Women scientists were not as common or as well regarded as men in those days. She thought that if she disguised her gender, by using her initials instead of her full name in her communications, she might be taken more seriously. Even that didn't seem to help.

At last, she heard about Jakes Ewer, a professor in South Africa. He knew of a cattle farmer who had giraffes roaming on his ranch near Kruger National Park in South Africa. Then, in the mid-1950s, about one hundred giraffes lived within the park. Ewer wrote to the farmer, asking if a young scientist named A. C. Innis could stay at the ranch while studying giraffes. Assuming the guest was a man, the farmer agreed.

In May 1956, she embarked on a life-changing mission. She did not hesitate to travel alone, and she paid her own way. From her base at the ranch, she spent nearly a year (1956–1957) studying giraffes in the wild, something no one—man or woman—had ever done before. She was the first person ever to do extended field research on a wild animal in Africa. She was not only a pioneer in her field. She was also a pioneering female biologist. Four years later, Jane Goodall began her studies of wild chimpanzees in Tanzania, and three years after that, Dian Fossey began her African work with the mountain gorillas of Rwanda.

Writing down everything she observed, Innis noted what the giraffes ate, where they walked, how they interacted with one another, how they drank, and how males necked with other males. (By swinging their necks at one another, male giraffes neck as part of a fight for dominance. It is seldom harmful, but the losing giraffe knows when he's been "out-necked" by the winner.) She was also able to study the anatomy of the gigantic creature while working with a giraffe carcass. Besides keeping a detailed journal of her findings and experiences, she filmed giraffes as they moved across the savanna.

When she was done with her research in Africa, she went to England, where she met and married British physicist Ian Dagg in 1957. Regardless of her expertise and intelligence, she often wasn't taken seriously as a female researcher and college instructor. But she decided to earn a PhD from the University of Waterloo in Ontario, Canada. She wrote her dissertation using material she had gathered and studied from the giraffe films she had recorded while in Africa. Through it all, her love for giraffes never waned.

Anne Innis Dagg has written several books about her work with giraffes, including *Smitten by Giraffe: My Life as a Citizen Scientist*, published in 2016. The book looks at Dagg's research and discusses the gender discrimination that she and other women in the sciences face.

Over the next six decades, Anne Innis Dagg has continued to research every aspect of the giraffe—anatomy, geographic ranges, movement, social behavior, differences among giraffe subspecies, and more. She has published several papers and books about giraffes. She has studied giraffes in the wild and in captivity, focusing on giraffes at the Taronga Zoo in Sydney, Australia. Observing how they interact, she notes that giraffes in zoos do not behave like giraffes in the wild. In the twenty-first century, Dagg is viewed by many as the Jane Goodall of giraffes. Her groundbreaking work opened the door not only to women in science but also to others who find the giraffe as fascinating as she does.

WORKING WITH THE DEAD

Before Dagg began studying giraffes, science was able to determine *what* the giraffe is—a tall ungulate (hoofed animal) common to the savannas of Africa. But it didn't go much further than that. Biologists didn't know the answers to the *hows* and the *whys* of the creature's life and behavior. Dagg says,

> The giraffe was not the only common animal whose life history was ignored up to the 1950s. The life history of virtually all animals was unknown. Zoologists were busy in the first half of the [twentieth] century naming and cataloguing species, and studying animal physiology and anatomy in the laboratory. It was easier to measure the leg of a dead giraffe than to trail a live animal through thorn thickets to watch the way the leg moved. It was easier to sit and measure a giraffe's canine tooth than to tramp over hot fields documenting the diet that affected the tooth's evolution. The reason why we know little about giraffe is clear, and just as obvious, I think [was] the need for me to rectify the gap in our knowledge.

Throughout the last half of the twentieth century, many people, including some conservationists and zoologists, assumed the giraffe population was holding steady. Keeping track of giraffes in the wild is not easy. Their range is enormous, covering hundreds of miles. Were observers in the wild seeing the same groups of giraffes or different ones? It was difficult to know for sure.

DISCOVERING THE SILENT EXTINCTION

The rapid decline in the overall giraffe population went unnoticed by almost everyone—except for the few giraffe experts in the field. In the background, a mostly unnoticed tragedy was unfolding. As giraffes slowly sauntered across the savannas of Africa, their numbers were dropping season by season, year by year.

Other animals made big news, animals with dramatic and heartbreaking stories of slaughter and destruction on a sometimes-massive scale. Reports and documentaries kept the public informed about

- poachers killing elephants for their tusks
- rhinos being slaughtered for their horns
- humans hunting wild cats, especially lions and tigers
- conflicts between farmers and cheetahs, leading to a critical loss of cheetah populations in the wild
- massive numbers of dolphins and porpoises caught in commercial fishing nets, leading ultimately to their deaths from infection

Even as those stories were capturing the public's attention, scientists and conservationists thought giraffes were safe. Based on data for the 1994 (2.3) version of the Red List, scientists categorized the giraffe in 1996 as lower risk of extinction. Twelve years later, in 2008, giraffes' status was still unremarkable, labeled as Least Concern. The radical decline in giraffe populations lay hidden. But not for long.

Experts in the field had begun to suspect that giraffe populations were falling. They got busy using new, more accurate methods to collect data. As biologists in Africa and around the world began to analyze the new data and information, an alarming picture of giraffes in the wild emerged. The data focused on two subspecies of giraffes—the West African giraffe and the Rothschild's giraffe. Many giraffe experts and organizations combined their discoveries.

OF LIONS AND BABY GIRAFFES

Giraffes have few predators, but lions, leopards, spotted hyenas, and sometimes cheetahs and crocodiles come after young giraffes. Lions will sometimes attack adults as well. Because they are easy prey, about 50 percent of newborn giraffes die before they are one year old.

A recent study by Zoe Muller of the Rothschild's Giraffe Project in Kenya showed that where lions and giraffes coexist, giraffe populations may have a tough time increasing. Muller reported that the main cause of death for giraffe calves was lion predation. Young giraffes are a lion's preferred target and almost never survive an attack. Unless young giraffes are able to survive into adulthood to reproduce, the population will face an uphill battle to increase. Muller recommends limiting the number of lions in protected areas where giraffes reside.

Large predator animals target giraffe calves, such as this young West African giraffe (*Giraffa camelopardalis peralta*) in Niger.

They included governments of African nations where giraffes live, nongovernmental organizations such as the Giraffe Conservation Foundation, universities, the IUCN, and independent researchers. A group within the IUCN—the Species Survival Commission Giraffe and Okapi Specialist Group—became responsible for compiling the various reports, information, and data. The group then submitted its findings. (The okapi is in the same taxonomic family—Giraffidae—as the giraffe.) That data became the basis for the conservation status assessment and Red List updates for giraffes that the IUCN issued in 2008 and 2010. The numbers of West African giraffes and Rothschild's giraffes were so critically low at the time that the IUCN Red List categorized them as Endangered. Then they looked at the other giraffe subspecies.

In December 2016, the IUCN published a report on all giraffe subspecies in the wild, based on the data compiled and analyzed by the Species Survival Commission Giraffe and Okapi Specialist Group. The results stunned the conservation world.

The report announced that only 97,500 giraffes exist in the wild, a drop of 40 percent in only thirty years. The information spread quickly, as journals, magazines, newspapers, online resources, and television stations published news of the dramatic decline. In 2016 the British Broadcasting Corporation in the United Kingdom and the Public Broadcasting Service in the United States worked together to create an award-winning documentary, *Giraffes: Africa's Gentle Giants*, narrated by naturalist and journalist David Attenborough. Through

Low population numbers of the Rothschild's giraffe in the wild led conservationists to study the population of other giraffe subspecies. They discovered an alarming downward trend of numbers across many giraffe subspecies.

this film, the public learned more about giraffes and their quiet walk toward extinction.

Critical news continues to come from experts who evaluate giraffes in their natural habitats, providing alarming evidence of the dangers the animals are facing. Knowing the numbers of the species is just a starting point. The most telling facts come from taking a look at each region and each subspecies.

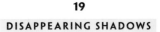

CHAPTER 2

TRACKING DOWN THE NUMBERS

In the early eighteenth century, most of the world's best scientific minds lived in Europe. They did not go to other countries or continents to study animals in their natural habitats. Scientists stayed in their offices and laboratories and relied on the observations of travelers who kept detailed journals and sketches of what they saw on their journeys. Studying animals from a distance had many limitations, especially when experts were using amateurs' observations to understand an entire species of animal.

Soon after Carl Linnaeus earned his medical degree in 1735, the Swedish zoologist, botanist, and physician published *Systema Naturae (Systems of Nature)*. In this book, he laid out a brilliant concept of organizing and naming all plants and animals through a hierarchical structure that showed their similarities—and differences—from one another. Scientists recognize Linnaeus as the Father of Taxonomy, the science of identifying, naming, and classifying organisms. In Linnaeus's system, each type of plant

Biologists look at physical features to identify giraffe species. The pattern and color of the hide and the animal's ossicones (horns) are the main clues. All giraffes have at least two ossicones on the top of their heads, but the placement differs. Their hides also vary depending on the species. This giraffe is in Kruger National Park in South Africa.

• •

and animal is categorized across seven subgroups, from kingdom to species. For convenience, scientists use the genus and species names when referring to any particular plant or animal. This binomial (two-name) system is generally in Latin or Greek, with both terms italicized. The taxonomic names also have common names in English and other modern, spoken languages. For example, human beings are *Homo sapiens,* and giraffes are *Giraffa camelopardalis.*

Linnaeus observed many creatures in nature. But he had never seen live giraffes. When he came up with a name for this unusual species, he had to rely on illustrations and reports from travelers who had

NAME THAT ANIMAL!

Most experts agree that the word *giraffe* comes from the Arabic word *zarafa*. Some authorities say *zarafa* means "fast walker," while other linguists trace the meaning to "assemblage of animals." Both translations make sense to anyone who has watched the giraffe in its home territory. The ancient Greeks saw the animal as a hybrid of more than one creature, much like the mythological creatures in Greek mythology. The mythological Pegasus, for example, is part horse and part bird. When ancient Greeks first saw a giraffe, they named it the camel leopard. Its body resembled a camel, but it had spots like a leopard, two animals with which the Greeks were very familiar. That is how scientists came up with the taxonomic name for the species: *Giraffa camelopardalis. (Camelopardalis* is the Latinized word from the Greek that means "camel marked like a leopard.")

seen them in Egypt in northern Africa. Like most people at the time, Linnaeus assumed that all giraffes in Africa were the same species, spread out over other territories. So he grouped them all into one species under the scientific name *Giraffa camelopardalis.*

Toward the end of the eighteenth century, a French traveler and ornithologist named François Le Vaillant set off for Africa to collect specimens of birds and other animals. Unlike other travelers before him, he decided to trek across southern Africa, far from Egypt where giraffe samples had been curated and sent to Europe. Le Vaillant kept a written record of his visit, describing in detail the wildlife he saw. He also had some giraffes killed so he could send the bones and hides to Europe for others to study.

Enter French zoologist Étienne Geoffroy Saint-Hilaire nearly one hundred years later. He had examined Le Vaillant's writings and giraffe specimens, but he also had another specimen to investigate. In 1827 Saint-Hilaire had the honor of leading a giraffe, a gift to the king of France, from the French port city of Marseille to Paris. This giraffe looked decidedly different from the lifeless samples he'd been studying. He suspected that there might be two species instead of one. Some biologists agreed with him, but most held the more accepted understanding of one species, *Giraffa camelopardalis.* In the twenty-first century, zoologists and biologists still categorize giraffes under one species, with nine subspecies.

Often scientific information is not set in stone, and new information leads experts to reevaluate earlier theories and practices. For example, an early twentieth-century zoologist named Richard Lydekker of the British Museum in London began to study giraffe specimens from all over Africa. He recognized that giraffes were not all the same, identifying various subspecies, depending on where the animals lived and what they looked like. Most of the subspecies names, which are still used, come from Lydekker.

Like Saint-Hilaire, Lydekker realized from studying giraffe samples that there were at least two separate species of giraffes. Rather than using geography (information about where the giraffes came from) for this conclusion, Lydekker separated the two species by their distinctive skin patterns. He called giraffes with a blotched pattern of spots *Giraffa camelopardalis.* He named those with a netted skin pattern of well-defined light, thin lines surrounding different-sized spots *Giraffa reticulata,* or the reticulated giraffe.

Other giraffe studies followed in the 1930s, 1960s, and 1990s. These investigations concurred that the one species and nine subspecies taxonomy was more accurate. It remains the IUCN Species Survival Commission Giraffe and Okapi Specialist Group's recognized taxonomy.

GETTING TO KNOW THEM

Most people think that one giraffe pretty much looks like any other giraffe. That is probably because most of us have only seen giraffes at zoos, and the giraffe most commonly found in US zoos is the *Giraffa reticulata.*

TAXONOMY

How can you make sense of a vast array of living things? Just like you make sense of your messy closet: you organize things.

How can you make sure people who speak different languages are talking about the same creature? You choose a language that every scientist recognizes: Latin.

Linnaeus's taxonomy system is a good way—though not perfect—to create order from Earth's wildly diverse world of plants and animals. The system is organized into seven main categories:

- kingdom
- phylum
- class
- order
- family
- genus
- species

The animals in each category are similar in increasingly specific ways. Giraffes, for example, as animals, are grouped with all other animals in the kingdom Animalia. Giraffes are also mammals, so they are grouped with other mammals in the class Mammalia.

Linnaeus classified more than twelve thousand species of plants and animals. He shared his new system in his books *Species Plantarum (The Species of Plants,* 1753) and *Systema Naturae (System of Nature,* 1758). Scientists still consult these books.

Besides naming living things, taxonomy helps biologists identify which organisms are native to an area and which are not. Invasive species are those that can take over an area that is not their native territory. Often invasive species enter a new area because humans take them there, accidentally or on purpose. Scientists use taxonomy to identify which species belong to an environment and which ones are intruders. For example, cane toads *(Bufo marinus)* are not native to the United States. Sugarcane farmers imported these toads from Central and South America to eat the white grubs that were destroying their crops. This huge amphibian looks a lot like Florida's native, the southern toad *(Bufo terrestris)*. The cane toads reproduce by the thousands and have overrun much of Florida. They eat all the native species of frogs, toads, and even pet food. Worst of all, cane toads are poisonous. This is only one example of a dangerous invasive species that can destroy native species and their habitats.

By labeling plants and animals, taxonomy also provides a structure for keeping track of the biodiversity of our planet. Scientists and conservationists work together to monitor the health of various species, if and how they are evolving, and how threatened by the possibility of extinction they might be. Taxonomists continue to add to the list of known species. They make changes to a creature's taxonomy when new scientific evidence proves such a change is necessary. To date, taxonomists have named about 1.8 million distinct species of plants and animals. Scientists estimate that at least 7 million more are waiting to be discovered and given a taxonomic name.

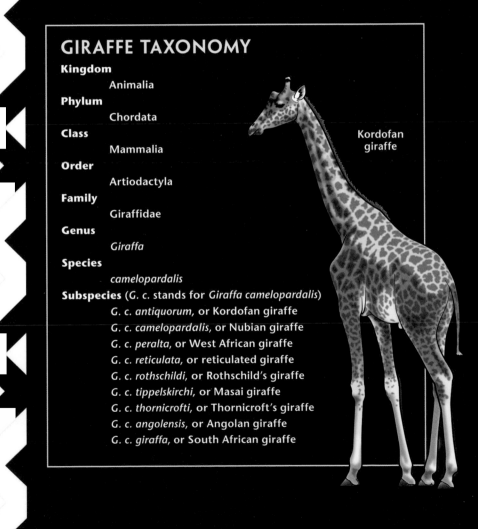

GIRAFFE TAXONOMY

Kingdom
Animalia
Phylum
Chordata
Class
Mammalia
Order
Artiodactyla
Family
Giraffidae
Genus
Giraffa
Species
camelopardalis
Subspecies (*G. c.* stands for *Giraffa camelopardalis*)
G. c. antiquorum, or Kordofan giraffe
G. c. camelopardalis, or Nubian giraffe
G. c. peralta, or West African giraffe
G. c. reticulata, or reticulated giraffe
G. c. rothschildi, or Rothschild's giraffe
G. c. tippelskirchi, or Masai giraffe
G. c. thornicrofti, or Thornicroft's giraffe
G. c. angolensis, or Angolan giraffe
G. c. giraffa, or South African giraffe

Kordofan giraffe

THE OKAPI

At first glance, the okapi (*right*) looks like a hybrid of a zebra and a deer. This shy creature is not directly related to either animal. Scientists believe the prehistoric *Zarafa zelteni,* whose fossils were found in Libya, was the okapi's ancestor. Okapis and giraffes are the only living members of the Giraffidae family in the world. Unlike giraffes, which live in several regions of Africa, okapis live only in the Ituri Rainforest of the Democratic Republic of the Congo in central Africa.

Because they live in the rain forest, okapis have adapted to help them survive there. For example, they have an oily coat that allows heavy rains to run off. Okapis have excellent hearing and can move each ear independently, and their sense of smell is excellent. This helps them detect leopards, their main predator, which are hard to see in the dim light of the rain forest. And just as spots help camouflage leopards, the striping on an okapi's legs serve as camouflage in the forest's streaking sunlight and shadows.

The okapi has some direct similarities to its giraffe cousin. First, the male okapis have ossicones on their heads. All okapis have long, dark blue, prehensile (grasping) tongues, which they use like giraffes do to strip leaves from plants. Their tongues are so long, about 18 inches (46 cm), that they can clean their own eyes and ears with them! Both the giraffe and the okapi have the same number of vertebrae in their necks: seven.

We don't know much about okapis. The average life span of an okapi in the wild is unknown. In captivity, they typically live fifteen to thirty years. Female okapis give birth to one calf each. The calves spend their first few months hidden in the underbrush while their mothers feed on nearby plants.

The IUCN Species Survival Commission Giraffe and Okapi Specialist Group, led by Julian Fennessy, is studying and monitoring okapis in the wild. The okapi population is declining at an alarming rate. In 2013, after a new assessment, the IUCN changed the okapi's Red List status from Near Threatened to Endangered. The main causes of its decline are forest loss, hunting, human population growth, armed conflict, and lack of protection by local government. Some okapi-specific conservation efforts are underway. But unless those efforts can reduce or eliminate the threats to the okapi, the animal could become extinct.

The differences among giraffe subspecies isn't always easy to recognize. Biologists look at three key physical features to identify a giraffe subspecies: the hide pattern and colors, the ossicones (horns), and the legs. Even experts find that some subspecies look very much alike, while individual

giraffes within a species can sometimes vary considerably. The most distinctive difference is also the largest: the giraffe's skin. Some subspecies have large, geometric spots, while others have smaller, very uneven splotches that resemble tree leaves. The spots also vary in color, from dark reddish brown to soft tan. The borders around the spots may be thick or thin, from cream-colored to nearly white. Scientists use skin pattern to identify a specific giraffe, because—like humans' fingerprints—no two giraffes' patterns are alike. While all giraffes have at least two ossicones, the number and placement on their heads differ. Most males have a third one, a median ossicone, in the center of the forehead. When all else fails, scientists look at the legs. Some subspecies' spots continue all the way to the hooves, but others fade into near white from the upper thigh down. Still other giraffes look as if they're wearing white knee socks because the spots stop at the knees.

KEEPING TRACK OF THE GENTLE GIANTS

By far the best way of distinguishing one type of giraffe from another is by knowing its home territory. Each of the nine subspecies lives in a particular area of Africa, with minimal overlapping. Giraffes in the wild live in eastern, southern, central, and western Africa. The dry lands of the Sahara cover much of northern Africa and cannot support giraffe life.

According to the IUCN, giraffe populations are increasing in southern and western Africa but are decreasing in eastern and central Africa.

In evaluating the environmental health of giraffes, conservationists focus on the actual number of individual giraffes within each subspecies. If a subspecies has a large, increasing population, scientists believe it will do well over time, even in the face of drought, disease, or war. But if a subspecies' overall numbers are small, scientists know that natural disaster, disease, or war could completely eliminate that subspecies.

For a long time, experts in the field were observing giraffe behavior rather than paying attention to how many giraffes were surviving in the wild. To observe giraffes, scientists used the most basic equipment, their eyes and binoculars, to watch and record the animals' activities in their natural habitat. While she was in Africa in the mid-1950s, Anne Innis Dagg used photography and motion-picture recording of the giraffes she found. She wrote detailed documentation of her evidence.

In later decades, wildlife experts flew in small airplanes and helicopters for a bird's-eye view of giraffes over a much larger territory. It was harder to distinguish individual giraffes from that vantage point, but the ability to cover hundreds of square miles in a short time was a real improvement. Even so, those methods were too expensive for regular population assessments.

How do wildlife experts keep track of and count individual giraffes in the twenty-first century? New technologies are helping. You might think that putting a collar on a giraffe's long neck would make sense. In 2001–2002, the Giraffe Conservation Foundation did exactly that. In a trial program, the foundation placed collars that could be tracked by global positioning satellite (GPS) technology on giraffes in Namibia. In 2010 newer camouflaged neck collars also included GPS tracking devices. Using a neck collar on a giraffe didn't quite work out. Giraffes are plant eaters, or herbivores, that browse, eating leaves from high branches and large bushes. Some giraffes were injured when their collars became tangled while they were eating. Other giraffes threw off

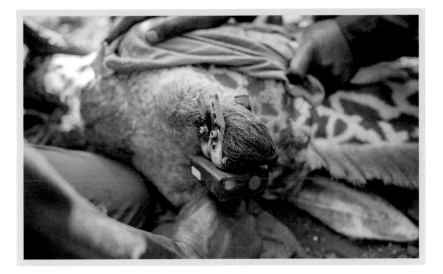

Researchers attach a small solar-powered satellite tracker to a giraffe's ossicone. The tracker records the animal's GPS position once every hour.

their collars—an expensive loss of material and time. Wildlife experts knew they needed to develop a more effective tracking device.

Eventually, GPS tracking devices became much smaller. Rather than using a neck collar, some experts used a head harness with a GPS attachment. These didn't work out well either, because they limited the giraffes' head movement and ability to eat.

Wildlife experts have moved on to a much smaller solar-powered satellite tracker that they can mount around a giraffe's ossicone. In June 2017, these ossi-units were placed on eleven reticulated giraffes in Kenya. Every day, the ossi-units relay information about the animals' locations, hour by hour.

To place one of these units on a giraffe, a team has to work carefully. First, they dart the giraffe with a sedative. The crew then helps the lofty, lumbering animal safely to the ground. Once the animal is down, a crew member places a cloth over its eyes. Everyone works fast. If a giraffe is sedated for more than about thirty minutes, it can die. That is because the sedation lowers the animal's heart rate, or beats per minute. Lower beats per minute pushes less oxygen-carrying blood up the animal's long neck and into its brain. Too much time under sedation equals too little oxygen and possible brain damage or even death for the giraffe. A team member must quickly attach a unit to one of the ossicones. The procedure takes about ten minutes. The animal regains consciousness, and the team stands by to be sure it recovers from sedation. As the animal heads off, the unit will track it for two years—or until the unit fails.

The information the tracking devices gather is sent by satellite every hour to the researchers' computers. Wildlife experts assess the data to learn about giraffes' ranges, the kind of habitat they seem to like best and return to, and changes in their movement during wet and dry seasons. Healthy habitats are critical to giraffe survival. So conservationists work to learn more about where giraffes travel at different times of the year. This helps to develop plans to protect and preserve those habitats in the wild.

Julian Fennessy, cofounder of Giraffe Conservation Foundation, says that the giraffe data "[helps] us to understand the expanding population better and the extent of their range as they move into new frontiers. In turn, this will enable us to educate the local communities and help them to understand the importance of preserving the giraffe."

THE DOWNSIDE OF TRACKING DEVICES

Tracking devices do have a few downsides. First, each costs $2,500, and organizations don't always have enough funds to pay for them. Each tracking expedition takes several people, many hours, and a lot of money—at least another $2,500. Second, the risks of sedating a giraffe so it can be fitted with a device are high. The animal may be injured—or it could die. Finally, scientists can only collar and track a limited number of giraffes using ossi-units.

Experts use another technology to keep track of giraffes: the camera. A digital camera is one of the most important tools in a conservationist's bag of equipment. Software developers have created a GiraffeSpotter program—with support from the San Diego Zoo Global and Giraffe Conservation Foundation. Every giraffe has its own spot shapes and patterns, which do not change, much like the way each person has a distinct set of fingerprints. The software is similar to facial recognition software on cell phones and computers, and it can recognize the unique coat patterns of each giraffe. Scientists and conservationists can feed photos into the program, creating a database of visual information about the giraffes they are tracking. They can follow individual giraffes throughout their lives.

According to the Giraffe Conservation Foundation's Stephanie Fennessy, photos are a helpful way of identifying giraffes. She says, "Photo IDs can be done 'manually' by looking at ID photos and comparing them or with the help of a photo recognition program. This is done to get exact population numbers, and in some cases, to learn more about social networks of giraffes—who hangs out with whom." Photos also offer another benefit: no darts, no collars, no danger.

Wildlife experts are working hard to protect, preserve, and improve giraffes' lives and habitats. They use science, technology, and ingenuity to learn as much as they can—and they've discovered some surprises along the way.

CHAPTER 3
SCIENCE HAS SOME SURPRISES

New scientific knowledge never stands on its own. It is supported by centuries of previous observation, experimentation, and critical thinking. We are continually learning new and sometimes surprising things about the universe, our planet, and the creatures with whom we share Earth. Even so, as much as we do know, there's still much that we don't know.

For a long time, giraffes in the wild had not been studied closely. Then Anne Innis Dagg opened the door to giraffe biology and behavior in the 1950s. It's been a slow crawl to build a body of knowledge.

Wildlife experts are the first to declare that they still don't know as much about giraffes as they would like to know to help the animals survive. Some of the basic information they once assumed to be true is being reevaluated. New observations, technologies, and scientific tools are uncovering some surprises about the gentle giants.

During mating season, male giraffes use their necks to dominate one another in the struggle to impress and win a female mate. Scientists call this display of dominance necking.

Scientists do agree on some very basic facts about giraffes.

HEIGHT OF AN AVERAGE ADULT
- Male: 17 feet 4 inches (5.3 m), the tallest ever recorded—more than 19 feet (5.8 m)
- Female: 14 feet 2 inches (4.3 m)

WEIGHT OF AN AVERAGE ADULT
- Male: 2,000 pounds (907 kg), the heaviest ever recorded—more than 4,200 pounds (1,905 kg)]
- Female: 1,800 pounds (816 kg)

LIFE SPAN: about 25 years

RATIO OF MALES TO FEMALES: almost even (1:1)

SLEEP: 4.5 hours, mainly at night, standing or lying down

DIET: tree leaves, fruit, pods, shoots, and rarely grass

FEEDING: browsing, using the upper lip and prehensile tongue to grasp food

SENSES: color vision, acute sense of smell, and good hearing

GESTATION (PREGNANCY): about 15 months (453 to 464 days)

OFFSPRING: a calf (rarely twins) that falls to the ground at birth and stays with its mother for up to 22 months

WHAT ABOUT THAT LONG-NECK THEORY?

One of the oldest questions and often the first one most people wonder about is, Why the long neck? No other animal has a neck close to the length of the giraffe's, and none is nearly as tall. Fossil records show that the giraffe's neck evolved over time. Two main theories explain why it happened.

The giraffe is one of the most used examples in Charles Darwin's theory of evolution. He explained the long neck as evidence of adaptation. Many scientists have agreed and have used the giraffe's unique neck length to explain how, over a long time, this species gradually evolved, or changed and adapted, to stretch higher and higher to reach the best, tenderest leaves on the tall trees. Way up high, the giraffe had no competition in the treetops. While other animals foraged low in the grasses and bushes around the giraffes' knees, the towering fellows had the best food all for themselves. Experts in the field in Africa still observe this browsing behavior among giraffes, and they support the food-based theory of giraffe-neck evolution.

Not everyone agrees. Others have observed giraffes eating just as much from lower branches and shoulder-high bushes. They contend that female giraffes, in particular, spend more time feeding with their necks horizontal to the ground than stretched upward foraging in treetops. These scientists also question why the giraffe neck didn't stop evolving when the animal reached 10 feet (3 m) high. The animal's upper-tree foraging would be just as successful if they were 4 to 6 feet (1.2 to 1.8 m) shorter. Some biologists have a different explanation for this remarkable anatomy. They refer to it as necks for sex.

Anne Innis Dagg was one of the first people to observe and report on a dominance behavior among male giraffes referred to as necking. (Another dominance posture for male giraffes is to hold their heads as high as possible, stretching upward to show how long their necks are.) As with males in most species, the competition to attract and mate with a female in estrus (heat) compels them to come up with some sort of alluring display. For some creatures, it's a dance. For others, it may be a special song or sound. For many large animals, however, the display is a fight.

DID YOU KNOW?

GIRAFFES SPEND UP TO 75 PERCENT OF THEIR TIME EATING.

For many years, biologists thought that giraffes used their horns for fighting. But Dagg and others have observed that instead of head-to-head assaults, such as those in which rams and deer engage, giraffes battle with their necks. They sway side to side, striking each other with their massive necks. The larger the neck, the better the outcome for a male giraffe—he will win the female.

Males are usually unharmed during these bouts, but the loser knows when he's been beaten and wanders off, leaving the winner to woo the nearby female. This works out well for her, too, because scientists have determined that females prefer older, stronger

males with large necks.
Because these are the males
that successfully mate with
the females, the traits of
the larger, longer-necked
males are passed on
genetically to the offspring.
Over a long time, the genes
of the longer-necked ones
keep moving forward into new
generations, while the smaller-necked
males die off with no offspring to carry on
their traits. Possibly, one or both evolutionary theories are correct. But
they remain theory rather than fact.

Dominant male giraffes that win the necking fight earn the
privilege of doing something unusual among animals. Before mating,
the female lets him taste her urine. As the female urinates, the potential
mating male samples the liquid so he can tell if she's in heat, ready to
become pregnant. If he detects the unique taste of estrus hormone in
the urine, he will mate with her. If the taste of the hormone is absent,
so is the hormone itself. The male will lose interest and go on his way
to find another female.

OTHER LONG-NECKED NEWS

Regardless of how their necks have become so long, the advantages
of having a long neck are important for survival in Africa. Reaching
food sources that others can never touch is only one benefit. A
giraffe's eyes, high up in the air, have unobstructed views of the
terrain. Giraffes are always looking for potential threats, such as
movements in the grasses that could be lions on the prowl. And a
new finding is a bit of a surprise. The giraffe neck is a natural form of
air-conditioning.

In the hot climate of the African savanna, giraffes turn to face the sun so that the neck casts a long and cooling shadow over the animal's body.

The savannas of Africa are some of the hottest regions in the world. A mammal's body has to find ways to stay warm during cold nights and to cool off during the day. One way some mammals have evolved to manage temperature is in the shape of their ears.

Animals in cold regions have relatively small ears that are close to the head, where the body's warm blood helps maintain a safe body temperature. In hot climates, some mammals have very large ears. As the air passes over this broad area, it cools the skin and blood vessels, managing the temperature of the animal's entire body. While giraffes do have big ears, they aren't large enough to cool the entire body. Some zoologists believe that a giraffe's neck is the body's natural air conditioner.

A group of four zoologists from the United States, South Africa, and Australia measured sixty giraffes to calculate the surface area of each animal's body. They assumed that if an animal has more surface area, its skin—which is an organ—can radiate, or send out, more heat

SCIENCE HAS SOME SURPRISES

than animals with less surface area. If so, that animal could keep itself cooler than those with less surface area. Because the giraffe is such a large animal, the zoologists wanted to see if giraffe skin alone was able to regulate body heat. But while the skin does provide some heat regulation through sweat glands, mostly found beneath the spots, giraffes keep their cool under the strong African sun because of their necks.

What would you do to escape the heat outdoors? You'd look for some shade. Trees provide shade, and the air temperature of a shaded area is lower than an unshaded area. Giraffes instinctively know about shade and use their necks to create it for their bodies. When they are standing out in the open sun, they turn to face the sun. In this position, the neck naturally casts a long shadow over the animal's back. If its neck were shorter, only a small area of the body would benefit from the shadow. Possibly, the long-neck adaptation, which keeps the sun's heat off the giraffe's back, is an answer to why the giraffe got its long neck.

CAN YOU HEAR ME NOW?

Long known as the silent giraffe, the tall animal might hush up around people. Giraffes do snort and sneeze, but for a long time biologists believed it was impossible for them to make any significant sound because the animals have such long throats.

A long neck means a long throat. It takes a lot of air to force sound through a throat, even a short one. So biologists assumed that giraffes were not capable of making sounds that we humans can hear. Some experts thought that perhaps giraffes make infrasonic, or low-frequency, sounds that are so low that humans can't detect them.

DID YOU KNOW?

GIRAFFES' LUNGS HOLD A LOT OF AIR: 12 GALLONS (45 L). BY COMPARISON, HUMAN LUNGS HOLD ONLY 1.59 GALLONS (6 L).

In 2015 biologists from Vienna, Austria, recorded giraffes in three European zoos. They evaluated more than one thousand hours of giraffe sound recordings. And they heard something. The sound was soft and low and soothing. And it happened only at night. The giraffes were humming! "I was fascinated, because these signals have a very interesting sound and have a complex acoustic structure," says Angel Stöger, one of the biologists at the University of Vienna.

No one knows why giraffes hum. One possibility is that humming is how giraffes let other giraffes know where they are in the dark. The low-frequency sound could be their way of saying, "I'm here." Another explanation is that it's a passive noise, a noise that is not made on purpose and often without awareness by its source, like snoring. However, giraffes take short power naps throughout the day and night, for a total of only about two hours. Snoring occurs only in the deep sleep that comes from longer sleep sessions, which is uncommon for giraffes. So, if it is a passive sound, it must be something else. Scientists want to do more research to understand why giraffes hum at night.

Some scientists, such as Zoe Muller—founder of the Rothschild's Giraffe Project in Kenya—believe that giraffes feel and express emotions, such as grief. This mother giraffe and her newborn in Kenya stay close for safety and for bonding.

DO GIRAFFES GRIEVE FOR THEIR DEAD?

Scientists hotly debate whether some animals, including giraffes, experience specific emotions such as grief. Giving human characteristics to nonhuman animals—anthropomorphism—is not something scientists encourage. "'Grieving' is a word that is perceived as illegal among scientists," says biologist Giovanni Bearzi of Dolphin Biology and Conservation at the University of Padua in Italy. "Our capability of understanding what happens from an animal's standpoint is pretty limited."

Still, it's hard to deny that some creatures, especially those that are highly social, display behaviors that look like grief when one of their group has died. For decades, scientists have observed this behavior in elephants, dolphins, gorillas, chimpanzees, polar bears, whales, and now in giraffes.

Zoe Muller, wildlife biologist and founder of the Rothschild's Giraffe Project in Kenya, described what happened as she was observing giraffes one morning in 2010. She noticed a group of seventeen female giraffes acting strangely in a part of the area where they seldom hung out. Muller drove to the area to get a closer look at what was going on.

The giraffes looked distressed, running chaotically, but instead of moving away from the area, they stayed there for two days. Muller recognized one of the adult females as a giraffe she had identified as F008. That female had recently given birth to a calf that had a deformed hind leg. Usually mothers leave their calves hidden in high grasses, where they are safe from predators. The mothers then browse nearby. From time to time, they return to nurse the calves. Yet F008 did not leave her calf. When Muller drove closer to the group of giraffes, she saw that F008's calf lay dead on the ground. Muller moved farther away, and over the next few days, she observed the females. They sniffed at and nuzzled the newborn's carcass, nudging it as if to try to wake it up. After two days, all the giraffes left except one—the calf's mother.

F008 stood guard, alone, over the body of her calf, alert to everything around her. She did not eat or drink at all, which is highly unusual for a giraffe. Each night predator hyenas ate away at the carcass, and by the fifth day, it was gone. Only then did F008 move on.

Muller believed that the mother was displaying grief, but she hesitated to call it that because "some scientists are very strict about not anthropomorphizing." Years later, she feels differently. "I would now be a lot more open about acknowledging nonhuman grief," she says. "Giraffes, humans, we're all mammals. Our system of emotion is largely driven by hormones, and hormones are likely to have evolved similarly in all mammals."

Scientists have begun to study hormone levels of some species

before and after losing a close family member. Anne Engh is working with baboons, and Bearzi is studying dolphins. Bearzi says, "As a human being, I can easily relate to animals' suffering because another animal died. And maybe it is not so complicated. Maybe it does have to do with the kind of grieving that we humans feel. It may not be exactly the same, but it looks like it is related."

GNAW ON THIS BEHAVIOR

In 2017 a wildlife ranger observed giraffes in South Africa nibbling at the bones of carcasses—as well as antlers, horns, and elephant ivory. Why would a plant eater choose to eat the bones of an animal? While it might seem surprising, it's not really. It's a behavior known as osteophagia (the chewing, eating, or both of bones by plant eaters). It's a specific kind of pica, or eating of nonfood items. The reason makes sense: the animal is under some kind of nutritional stress.

Giraffes scrape their teeth over the bones and don't usually swallow them. They chew and suck on the piece, and their saliva dissolves the surface of the bone, releasing calcium and other nutrients in the bone. Other herbivores do this too, including camels and cattle. Some zoologists think the giraffe is just bored, and gnawing on a bone gives it something to do.

THE BIGGEST NEWS: DNA DISCOVERY

Perhaps the most groundbreaking research of all is happening at the cellular level. For centuries most scientists grouped all giraffes under one species, *Giraffa camelopardalis*. As biologists began to find and compare giraffes from different regions of Africa, they subdivided each of those groups into subspecies.

A subspecies is an additional level of differentiation within a species. For example, all brown bears are the species *Ursus arctos*. The grizzly bear, *Ursus arctos horribilis*, is a subspecies of the brown bear.

(*Horribilis* designates the subspecies.) The polar bear, *Ursus maritimus,* is a separate species of bear. It is distinct from the brown bear, even though they are both big bears.

Most subspecies can successfully breed with one another but generally do not because of geographic range. The brown bear does not live where the polar bear lives, so they do not usually breed with each other in the wild. But some zoos in Europe have mated subspecies and have produced hybrid animals that are healthy and fertile. With climate change, the polar bear may have to expand its territory to survive, moving south into the brown bear's domain. These species may then begin to mate and produce offspring. But a hybrid is not a subspecies yet.

Deoxyribonucleic acid, or DNA, is the genetic material that determines the physical traits of every creature—how it will look and how it will function. DNA research is helping scientists solve the puzzle of how many giraffe species and subspecies exist.

Around 2001 the Giraffe Conservation Foundation started gathering skin samples from more than five hundred giraffes for DNA studies. Then scientists could look deeper than skin patterns, ossicones, and geographic boundaries to find, at a cellular level, what distinguishes one group of giraffes from another. Julian Fennessy worked with Axel Janke, a geneticist at the Senckenberg Biodiversity and Climate Research Centre in Frankfurt, Germany, to decode the DNA from the skin samples. In 2016 they announced the stunning results.

Fennessy reported that the DNA research showed not one (or two or three) but four giraffe species and five subspecies. According to Fennessy, the four species have been distinct and separate for more than one million years. Each of the groups lives in distinct areas of Africa. Even when some of the species and subspecies cross paths, they do not interbreed in the wild. They are as different as a brown bear and a polar bear.

SCIENCE HAS SOME SURPRISES

SPECIES: northern giraffe (*Giraffa camelopardalis*)
    SUBSPECIES: Kordofan giraffe (*G. c. antiquorum*)
                  Nubian giraffe (*G. c. camelopardalis*)
                  West African giraffe (*G. c. peralta*)

SPECIES: southern giraffe (*Giraffa giraffa*)
    SUBSPECIES: South African giraffe (*G. g. giraffa*)
                  Angolan giraffe (*G. g. angolensis*)

SPECIES: reticulated giraffe (*Giraffa reticulata*)
SPECIES: Masai giraffe (*G. c. tippelskirchi*)

With new DNA-based information, Fennessy and his team proposed this updated giraffe taxonomy.

• •

Two hundred years of giraffe taxonomy may have turned a corner. But it takes time for the scientific community to evaluate new findings, and the IUCN is reviewing the conclusions of the Giraffe Conservation Foundation's DNA study. "The number of species of giraffes has come in for much discussion and debate in recent years," the IUCN said in a 2017 statement. "The findings of this latest study will need to be carefully evaluated, as it could—as the authors note—have considerable implications for [giraffe] conservation. . . . If the findings of the current study are accepted, then it may well be that some species would be listed in the threatened categories on the IUCN Red List."

Fennessy says, "I would just hope that as the IUCN reviews this [study], they look at the fact [that] 200 years ago people looked at different coat patterns from [giraffe] samples sent from Africa and made a decision to call [the giraffe] one species and nine subspecies. And now, using . . . DNA, I think more science can help us answer the mystery." Fennessy believes that if his findings are formally accepted, three of the four species of giraffe would quickly be recategorized on the IUCN Red List as more seriously threatened.

WHY DOES THIS MATTER?

Dagg explains, "It is no longer enough to think that there are many thousands of giraffe[s] in national parks and reserves throughout Africa, so what is the problem? Instead, we must ensure that all genetic populations remain viable."

Zoe Muller, founder of the Kenya-based Rothschild's Giraffe Project, says, "Conservation is all about conserving biodiversity (i.e., genetic potential) and so understanding the genetic diversity of any species really is critical to enable us to conserve them properly. Of course, all the taxonomic divisions and classifications are something that [we] humans impose on nature as we try to categorize and understand our world, but it does offer an effective way of prioritizing areas which need attention, research/conservation funding, and raising awareness."

IT'S ALL ABOUT THE NUMBERS

The status of a species is based on accurate population counts in the wild. Usually the fewer individuals there are, the more critically endangered they may be. The estimated population of the species *Giraffa camelopardalis* as a single group is about one hundred thousand individuals in the wild. This doesn't seem dangerously low when experts compare that number with species that are labeled as Vulnerable, Threatened, and Endangered, such as the lion at twenty thousand, the cheetah at seventy-five hundred, or the mountain gorilla at 850 individuals. What if, instead of one giraffe species, science shows there are four? Suddenly the status of giraffes changes dramatically.

When conservationists apply the newly proposed DNA-based giraffe taxonomy to the animals' populations in the wild, the numbers tell a critical story. Each of the four separate species has far fewer individuals, few enough to warrant a change in their IUCN Red List status. The Giraffe Conservation Foundation's latest count in 2016 shows low numbers. For example, under its four-species taxonomy, the

COMPARATIVE THREATS

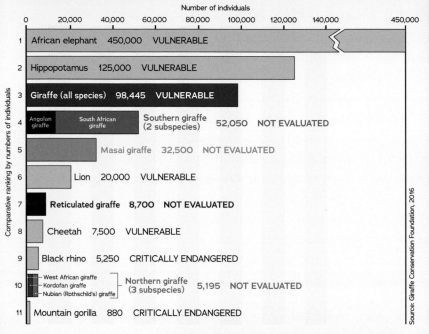

Number of individuals

Comparative ranking by numbers of individuals			
1	African elephant	450,000	VULNERABLE
2	Hippopotamus	125,000	VULNERABLE
3	Giraffe (all species)	98,445	VULNERABLE
4	Angolan giraffe / South African giraffe — Southern giraffe (2 subspecies)	52,050	NOT EVALUATED
5	Masai giraffe	32,500	NOT EVALUATED
6	Lion	20,000	VULNERABLE
7	Reticulated giraffe	8,700	NOT EVALUATED
8	Cheetah	7,500	VULNERABLE
9	Black rhino	5,250	CRITICALLY ENDANGERED
10	West African giraffe / Kordofan giraffe / Nubian (Rothschild's) giraffe — Northern giraffe (3 subspecies)	5,195	NOT EVALUATED
11	Mountain gorilla	880	CRITICALLY ENDANGERED

Source: Giraffe Conservation Foundation, 2016

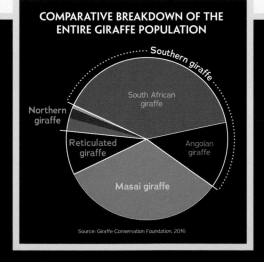

COMPARATIVE BREAKDOWN OF THE ENTIRE GIRAFFE POPULATION

Southern giraffe

South African giraffe

Northern giraffe

Reticulated giraffe

Angolan giraffe

Masai giraffe

Source: Giraffe Conservation Foundation, 2016

The infographic above, based on Convention on International Trade in Endangered Species (CITES) data, shows the numbers of giraffes in the wild, by species, in comparison to other large mammals in Africa. Although the threat level has not been evaluated for giraffes, the numbers are low and rank among those animals whose populations are vulnerable to extinction or critically endangered.

The infographic to the right ranks the numbers of giraffe subspecies. The South African and Masai giraffe populations, though low overall, are the highest of the giraffe subspecies. The three Northern giraffe subspecies have the lowest numbers.

foundation's count indicates that the northern giraffe has only 5,195 individuals, the reticulated giraffe 8,700, the Masai giraffe 32,000, and the southern giraffe 52,000. With these low numbers, the northern and reticulated giraffes would definitely qualify to be listed among the most endangered species on the planet.

Evidence that a subspecies is a species changes how governments, organizations, and experts approach conservation efforts. The new DNA research might help some giraffe species gain more attention and all-important funding if scientists determine these animals are facing extinction.

Regardless of the species and subspecies debate, the dire situation of giraffe survival is clear. More efforts are needed to protect and save the animals, and their IUCN Red List label goes a long way toward ensuring conservation resources for them.

CHAPTER 4

HABITAT LOSS AND FRAGMENTATION

The threats to giraffes in the wild are the same as for other large animals of Africa: loss and fragmentation of habitat, human conflicts (warfare), poaching (illegal hunting), ecological changes, and disease. Any one of those causes by itself can devastate a species and negatively impact its chances of survival. Giraffes face a combination of these factors, so their survival is in clear and present danger.

Africa is going through tremendous changes, and with those changes come opportunities and challenges. Considered one of the poorest continents, Africa is experiencing growth, with a population increase of about 5 percent each year. In contrast, annual population growth in the United States is less than 1 percent. Many African nations are modernizing to create improved standards of living for their inhabitants. As cities expand, they are building massive transportation and energy networks. They are also cashing in on natural resources such as gold, diamonds, and uranium to drive economic growth. These

Large private cattle farms in northwestern Kenya have driven away most of the area's wildlife, including giraffes. Indigenous herders, such as this member of the indigenous Samburu people, compete with private ranches over grasslands for their livestock to graze. The competition can sometimes become violent, especially during periods of intense drought when grasses die and the lives of the cattle—and their owners' livelihoods—are at stake.

changes are beneficial for many people, but they have negative impacts on the environment and wildlife.

COMPETING FOR RESOURCES

The causes for giraffe decline vary by region, but in every part of Africa where giraffes live, the loss of habitat is a serious problem. New human settlements, farmland, and industries broke up the large expanses of territory where the animals once roamed freely. To make way for these new developments, people cut down massive amounts of trees and shrubs in giraffe territory. Giraffes need to be able to walk across a large area to forage and be healthy. More buildings and infrastructures, more people, more vehicles, and more technology mean less room for wildlife. Although a rare occurrence, giraffes have been electrocuted when they walked into electrical lines that crossed their territories. Giraffes have also been killed by walking into the path of a moving train or vehicle.

The growing human population in Africa puts pressure on natural resources too. Nearly 90 percent of the people of Africa depend on wood as their main source of fuel for heating their homes and cooking their food. The landscape changes year by year as people cut down trees to meet their needs. This includes acacia trees, whose leaves are one of the primary sources of food for giraffes.

Cutting down trees, or deforestation, is also taking place to clear land for agriculture. Experts estimate that almost 90 percent of West Africa's forests have already been destroyed. Until recently, farmers and herders coexisted with giraffes without conflict over resources. They made a modest living running small farms or ranches. Then people arrived who wanted large ranches with many hundreds of head of cattle. These ranches cover many acres of land.

Livestock graze on grasses for food, stripping grasslands and leaving fewer food sources for wildlife such as antelope and wildebeests. Crop farmers have stripped the land of natural fauna—grasses, trees, and bushes—to plant staples, such as maize, or corn, and beans, in large fields. In Kenya crop farmers have also enlarged their fields to plant wheat. Wheat farming pays well—as much as 10,000 Kenyan shillings (about ninety-eight dollars) per acre per year, which is a good income for Kenyan farmers.

Loss of fauna reduces food resources for animals. And without the root structures of native plants to hold soil in place, the earth and its nutrients erode and wash away in wind and rainstorms. Over time, the land becomes a desert, and without enough water, plants and animals suffer.

Both cattle and crop farmers use fences to keep wildlife from trampling their crops. Fencing cuts off natural corridors that giraffes and other wildlife use to move across their range to find food and mates. The animals, which were once able to migrate over hundreds of miles, with trees in abundance, are forced to survive in much smaller territories. This is habitat fragmentation.

Zoologist and writer Jules Howard explains how habitat fragmentation weakens species and makes them more vulnerable to extinction:

> Giraffes are now split across Africa into discreet populations that no longer mix—they are nine isolated islands of life being increasingly squeezed from all sides. Mammoths, sabertooths and giant ground sloths (all non-African) [have] gone through similar such declines—isolated into breeding pockets, which were squashed, one by one, by encroaching threats like climate change, range competition and, in some cases, hunting by early humans. Nine small puddles will evaporate far more quickly than one big puddle, and so it is with life. It is the historic "death-by-a-thousand-cuts," writ large. Giraffes are just one striking addition to what is fast becoming a global phenomenon. It is the threat of fragmentation.

Farming brings another danger to the wildlife of Africa. Cattle carry dangerous diseases that can spread to giraffes and other animals. Giraffes and cattle are ungulates, so they tend to be susceptible to the same illnesses. Many of these diseases are transferred from one animal to another by insects, such as ticks and mosquitoes. Two of the worst, rinderpest and anthrax, spread easily from cattle to giraffes. So many giraffes in the Central African Republic and in Kenya have died from these diseases that they are still struggling to make a comeback.

THE MASAI MARA NATIONAL RESERVE IN KENYA

National reserves in various parts of Africa have dual goals: to protect wildlife and to encourage tourism, which brings in money. Tourists pay for the experience to see animals in their natural habitats. However, the influx of people into these protected areas increases competition between humans and wildlife for land and resources. The Masai Mara National Reserve in Kenya is one of Africa's most visited tourist destinations. Its popularity comes with an ecological price.

COUNTRY: Kenya

CAPITAL: Nairobi

SUBREGION: East Africa

SIZE OF COUNTRY: 224,081 sq. miles (580,367 sq. km)— five times the size of Ohio

SIZE OF PROTECTED AREAS: 8 percent

GIRAFFE SUBSPECIES: Masai giraffe *(G. c.* tippelskirchi*),* not assessed but may be plummeting; Rothschild's giraffe (*G. c. rothschildi*), Near Threatened; reticulated giraffe (*G. c. reticulata*), Endangered

SIZE OF RESERVE: 938 sq. miles (2,429 sq. km)

The Masai Mara National Reserve is in the southeastern corner of Kenya in East Africa. Tanzania is on its southern border. The reserve, named after the Maasai, an indigenous tribe, is an unfenced grassland in the northern part of the Serengeti savanna ecosystem. It is home to diverse wildlife, including elephants, lions, rhinos, buffalo, leopards, giraffes, zebras, and hippos. The 245-mile (395 km) Mara River runs north-south through the western region of the reserve. Each year more than one million wildebeests cross the river in late summer during the Great Migration.

The variety of wild animals in the reserve attracts tourists every year and brings an estimated $1.2 billion into the Kenyan economy. Yet with a heavy increase in wildlife tourism—four times what it was in the first decade of the twenty-first century—the reserve is facing critical problems. Some of the money from tourism goes to conservation. But it's not enough to make up for the damage done by the invasion of people into Kenya's precariously balanced ecosystems.

A mother giraffe and her calf (*Giraffa tippelskirchi*) cross a shallow river in the Masai Mara reserve.

• •

The Kenyan government spends tourism dollars on critical infrastructure: building roads, schools, and hospitals. But local governments tend to spend their income from tourists on things that encourage more tourism rather than on goods and services that help the local residents. While tourism does provide employment for some, those jobs tend to be menial, low-paying, and seasonal. Little of the income from tourists finds its way to the native Maasai population. To earn a living, the Maasai cut down trees to clear land for farming and sell charcoal they make by burning wood.

Lodges for tourists surround the reserve. Workers have erected miles of electric fences around the lodges to protect tourists from the same wild animals they have come to see. Yet these same fences create habitat fragmentation, cutting off and limiting the areas where wildlife can freely roam.

One of the main reasons for the population decrease in giraffes in the area has been the rapid expansion of human settlements along the edges of the reserve. Land value just outside of Masai Mara has skyrocketed, and wealthy investors are buying it up. Richard Branson, a world-renowned British businessperson and founder of the Virgin Group, has built a futuristic "camp" of domed tents with infinity pools where visitors can look out over the Masai Mara from their beds. People also find ways around the laws to buy land within the reserve, usually by bribing officials to give them land leases and permits.

Oxpeckers and giraffes have a symbiotic relationship that benefits both animals. The birds feast on harmful parasitic ticks that burrow into giraffe bodies to suck the mammal's blood.

OF OXPECKERS AND ARMPITS

Ticks and other insects can sometimes be beneficial to giraffes. Within any ecosystem, plants and animals interact in ways that support the lives of all species in that ecosystem. Giraffes are no exception. Some kinds of interaction are symbiotic, good for both creatures. In a symbiotic relationship, two different types of animals depend on each other for some aspect of their survival. Each organism benefits from the relationship. Giraffes have this kind of you-scratch-my-back-I'll-scratch-yours deal with yellow-billed oxpeckers.

Oxpeckers, sometimes called tickbirds, ride on large African mammals as they amble across the landscape. Like most furry animals, giraffes are hosts to different parasites. The parasite uses a host animal to meet some of its needs. The host gets nothing beneficial from the relationship. And the parasite can harm the host. It's the opposite of a symbiotic relationship. Case in point: mosquitoes and humans. Mosquitoes ingest our blood, and we get an itchy bump or even a disease such as malaria. One of the most common giraffe parasites is the tick.

Ticks burrow into a giraffe's skin and take nourishment from the host's blood. But not for long. Oxpeckers walk all over a giraffe's body, inspecting for ticks to grab with their yellow bills. It's not unusual to see a dozen or more of these birds hitching a ride on a single giraffe.

What happens to these birds at night? Do they fly away to nests and rejoin the animals at dawn? Camera traps in Tanzania's Serengeti National Park snapped some surprising photos one night. They showed some of the birds hanging out (literally) in a giraffe's armpit.

"You look at [the birds] on the giraffe, and they're just right up there," says Meredith Palmer, leader of a University of Minnesota study about the giraffe and oxpecker relationship. "It's a very safe, comfortable place for the birds. Once [they] find [a host], it's worth just sticking around so [the host] doesn't wander off."

Birds head to the trees to nest when they're ready to lay eggs. Once the eggs hatch, the birds come back to hitch a ride on the nearest giraffe until the next mating season.

MINING

Urbanization and farming are not the only causes of habitat loss. The African continent holds about 30 percent of the world's natural resources, much of it still untapped. These resources include valuable diamonds, gold, oil, natural gas, coal, iron, uranium, and cobalt. In some parts of Africa, mining is a major part of the economy. About 60 percent of the mining in Africa is gold mining. The continent is also well known for its diamonds. About 55 percent of all diamonds come from Angola, Botswana, the Central African Republic, and the Democratic Republic of the Congo.

HLUHLUWE-IMFOLOZI PARK IN SOUTH AFRICA

In southern Africa, tourism is taking a back seat to another income producer: mining. The oldest protected area on the continent, the Hluhluwe-iMfolozi Park, is one of the best game reserves on Earth. More rhinos live here than anywhere else. But nearby is an area rich in coal, and two mines are already operating. A third is planned.

The oldest protected area in Africa, the Hluhluwe-iMfolozi Park, is home to Africa's southern white rhinos. They were hunted to near extinction in the late nineteenth century—first by Zulu hunters and then by white hunters—until fewer than twenty remained in the wild. All of them lived in Hluhluwe. In 1895, after one hunter killed six white rhinos, the South African national government set aside the land as a game sanctuary, protecting the wildlife that lived there. Even protected lands are not safe from poachers. So rhino populations grew slowly. By the 1950s, fewer than one hundred white rhinos were left in South Africa. In the 1960s, the park established Operation Rhino, an ongoing successful conservation program. In the twenty-first century, about twenty thousand white rhinos live in South Africa, many of them descendants of those saved in 1895.

Many of the most popular wild animals are regularly spotted in the park area. They include giraffes and what are known as the Big Five game animals—lions, leopards, rhinoceroses (both black and white species), elephants, and Cape buffalo. That's the good news.

However, workers at two giant coal mines are busy digging, extracting, and moving coal just a few miles from the reserve. Previously a quiet, clean, beautiful area, it is rocked by the dynamite blasts that break up and loosen

COUNTRY: South Africa

ADMINISTRATIVE CAPITAL: Pretoria

SUBREGION: Southern Africa

SIZE OF COUNTRY: 470,693 sq. miles (1,219,090 sq. km)—slightly less than twice the size of Texas

SIZE OF PROTECTED AREAS: 14.1 percent

GIRAFFE SUBSPECIES: South African giraffe (G. c. giraffa), not assessed

SIZE OF RESERVE: 370 sq. miles (960 sq. km)

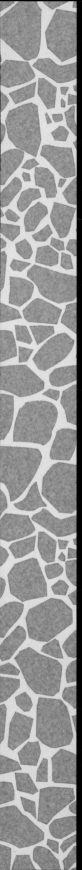

the compacted seams of anthracite, or coal. Plans for a third mine, the Fuleni mine, are underway for a site only 100 to 300 feet (30 to 91 m) from the park's southern border.

"Undoubtedly the noise, blasting, vibrations, and other side effects of the Fuleni mine will have a severe adverse impact on this world-famous wilderness area," says Morgan Griffiths of the Wildlife and Environment Society of South Africa. The other two mines are already driving away the area's wildlife and tourism because of the noise of blasting and the rumbling and bright lights from ever-moving coal trains at night.

Noise and light pollution are harmful enough, but air and water pollution add to the reserve's

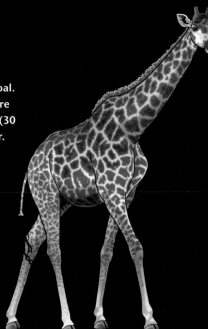

South African giraffe (*G.c. giraffa*)

problems. Coal dust floats through the air and is harmful to plants, animals, and people. A side effect of the mining is acid mine drainage. As water flows over the exposed mineral deposits, it picks up traces of acidic material. This water leaches, or seeps, from the mines into nearby water sources such as the White Umfolozi River. Plants, fish, and other wildlife cannot tolerate the change in the water's acidity, and they begin to die off. The drainage can devastate the food chain of a region.

Tour guide Nunu Jobe explains the tension between the park and the mines:

> We already have one of the best game reserves in Africa, with millions of tourists coming to the region to see the wild animals. We all need jobs, and the communities must benefit, but if there is another mine here, close to the park, then surely the government is telling people that our park jobs don't matter? There are hundreds of people working at Hluhluwe-iMfolozi, and these jobs will always be there if we look after the land and the wild animals. Unlike mining jobs, which will eventually disappear, leaving a damaged, useless land.

A WHITE GIRAFFE APPEARS

Giraffes blend in with their surroundings through their natural colors. And they stand so still that unless they move, predators don't see them. Herders in Kenya are used to seeing giraffes as they move their herds from area to area. Imagine the surprise one Kenyan villager felt in 2017 when he saw a rare, white reticulated giraffe mother (*below*) and her calf! He contacted Abdullahi H. Ali, founder of the Hirola Conservation Program in Kenya and the local conservation expert.

Ali was thrilled to be able to photograph and film the two giraffes. It was the first time video has captured these rare creatures. On his website, Ali wrote, "We spent almost twenty minutes with the beautiful animals. . . . To our surprise, one normal colored reticulated giraffe also was among the mother and calf. You can actually compare the difference." He noted that the calf had "tinges of color" that seemed to be "fading away, leaving the baby white as it approaches adulthood." He reported that the pair seemed to be in excellent health.

Ali and his colleagues quickly determined that the two giraffes have leucism, a partial loss of pigmentation in its skin, hair, feathers, or scales. (Leucism does not affect the eyes.) The condition is not the same as albinism, when pigmentation is missing and the eyes are red or pink. Both leucism and albinism happen in all species of animals and plants. Pale or perfectly white animals are often held in high esteem by indigenous groups, who sometimes hunt them because of their rarity. Ali and his team plan to monitor the white giraffes throughout their life spans and report their findings.

Companies from all parts of the world are scrambling to get their hands on Africa's mineral resources. So mining has expanded into more regions of Africa, often into remote and previously unexplored territories. Some mining has moved into protected areas—areas set aside for biodiversity conservation. For example, the United Nations Educational, Scientific and Cultural Organization had set aside the Selous Game Reserve in Tanzania in 1982 as a protected World Heritage Site. However, in 2012, UNESCO allowed the Tanzanian government to redraw the boundaries of the reserve, cutting out about 80 square miles (200 sq. km) to allow open-pit uranium mining. In open-pit mining, giant machines remove tons of dirt to get at minerals below, destroying the natural landscape and impacting the ecosystem it supports. The scars on the land remain, unless the mining company is obligated by contract to return the environment to its natural state.

Meanwhile, UNESCO and IUCN both sounded the alarm about the Tanzanian government's decision to construct a hydroelectric plant within the game reserve. To build the plant, the government would give logging rights to companies to build a giant dam that would provide the waterpower to produce electricity. The large-scale deforestation of this part of the reserve would be almost irreversible. Both organizations are urging the government to find better alternatives for electricity.

"Habitat loss, and fragmentation, may be the most potent factor in the decline of giraffe, and most other African wildlife. . . . Globally in the 21st century, habitat loss is the primary cause of species extinction and decline," writes environmentalist Bryan Shorrocks. "Sadly, intact African savannahs are increasingly only found in protected areas."

As wildlife and humans continue to compete for natural resources, conflicts arise—and wildlife usually loses the battle.

CHAPTER 5

HUMAN VIOLENCE AND CLIMATE CHANGE

War and violence are part of the human experience. Because animals coexist with us, they sometimes become casualties of human violence too. In any conflict, untold numbers of humans are killed and maimed, people struggle to find food and water, land is destroyed, and wildlife scatters. Even national parks and wildlife reserves are caught in the crossfire of war. Researchers report that 71 percent of protected areas in Africa have experienced conflict between 1946 and 2010. During these conflicts, humans killed many large mammals—elephants, hippos, giraffes, and others—for food and income. Humans killed animals such as elephants for highly valued animal parts, such as tusks to sell for ivory. The money from the sales on illegal black markets supports militaries as well as civilians.

A West African giraffe (*Giraffe camelopardis peralta*) eyes local villagers in the West African nation of Niger. Giraffes and other wild animals compete with humans for resources. Both are often victims of war. Although conflict is ongoing in some parts of Niger, the greatest threats to giraffes there are human population growth, hunting, climate change, and agricultural encroachment.

• •

Most of the residents of warring regions have no stake in the fight but must find ways to stay alive. Besides the danger of death from gunfire, they also face starvation, malnutrition, disease, and extreme poverty. Survival is their goal, and it's measured one day at a time through meeting the most basic needs: food, water, shelter, and life. They see the giraffe and other wildlife as a solution to some of these problems, so they kill the animals for food and sell what they do not eat. Some villagers help poachers find and kill animals, too, to earn money for themselves and their families.

Civil unrest is a key cause of the extinction of giraffes in some countries—and it's taking them to the edge of annihilation in others.

GIRAFFES AND CIVIL WAR IN ANGOLA

Angola is a nation in southwestern Africa. Angolans fought for their freedom from Portuguese colonial rule from 1961 to 1974. Civil war between government factions continued for another twenty-seven years. Armies placed land mines across the country, causing death and injury to both people and wildlife. About 1.5 million people were killed and another 4 million displaced.

National parks had no protection as the government focused on military efforts, not conservation. Angolan refugees who had lost their homes filled the nation's abandoned national parks. Relying on whatever they could hunt and gather, the refugees killed wildlife, including every Angolan giraffe, *G. c. angolensis,* for bushmeat. This subspecies became extinct in its native country.

After the civil war, the Angolan government reintroduced wildlife to the country's national parks. For example, in 2001, the Kissama Foundation started Operation Noah's Ark. The foundation translocated four South African giraffes, *G. c. giraffe,* from Madikwe Game Preserve in South Africa and introduced them into Angola's Kissama National Park. The most recent count in 2013 shows that this subspecies' population has increased from zero to twenty. Angolan giraffes are still extinct in this country.

POACHING

Poaching is illegal hunting. Governments can and do pass strong laws to protect endangered species, but unstable and impoverished countries often cannot control poaching within their borders. Poachers kill large wildlife to sell and to eat, but they also capture animals such as exotic birds and snakes to sell as pets. They also sell specific parts of animals, including ivory, horns, hides, organs, and meat.

Illegal buying and selling of wildlife (dead or alive) is wildlife trafficking. According to the World Travel and Tourism Council, "The world is facing an unparalleled spike in the illegal trade of wildlife,

A group of anti-poaching officials from Niger reach this victim before the poachers do. It could not be saved, so the officials will donate the meat to local villagers.

which is effectively endangering over 7,000 species in 120 countries around the globe. This multibillion-dollar industry cannot be ignored. It is the fourth most lucrative global crime, valued between $7 billion and $23 billion annually. What's more, only 3% of this revenue trickles down to the local communities."

International wildlife trafficking is growing. The high demand for rare items, even if buying and selling them is illegal, allows traffickers to charge enormous prices. This lucrative crime is also a violent one.

Poachers use two main methods for killing giraffes. Military groups and some individuals use rifles. Others use steel-wire snares to bring down the giraffes (and other wild animals that get caught in them). If the snares are placed at ground level, giraffes' feet get caught in the wires and they fall to the ground, where poachers kill them with machetes. Sometimes the wires are high in the trees, and giraffes get their necks tangled in the snares. These snares "pull tight around their necks or legs, causing strangulation and horrific wounds," says Richard Bonham, director of operations for Big Life Foundation in Kenya. "As the noose gradually tightens, it can take hours if not days for [the animal] to pass away." Either way, the poachers take what they want and leave the rest of the animal for the scavengers nearby.

Stephanie Romansch of the African Wildlife Conservation Fund in Zimbabwe agrees. "Snares are cruel. Animals often die lingering and painful deaths or they might break the snare and develop festering wounds that just don't heal. Poachers frequently set large numbers of snares and forget where they set them or just leave them in the bush, and what's the result? Large numbers of animals killed unnecessarily."

What giraffe parts are most in demand, and how are they used? The main reason giraffes are poached is for food. Poverty drives the demand for cheap food, and poaching costs nothing. In some African regions, bushmeat is a staple food for residents. Noelle Kumpel of the Zoological Society of London says, "Many of the threats to rhinos and elephants are the same for giraffes. The threats are local. It's loss of habitat and increasingly it's poaching, but not for the international trade. It's bush meat hunting."

One giraffe is the source of about 660 pounds (300 kg) of meat. Hunters sell the meat at markets and roadside stands for about half the local price of beef or lamb. Some poachers take the meat directly to a butcher shop, where the owners will sell it openly. Others sell it on the international market as an exotic meat.

Bonham says, "There is nothing new about 'bush meat' in Africa. Tribes have been hunter-gathering for centuries. Hunting traditionally, they revere the animals they take and only kill what they need to feed their families. Sadly, that's all changed. Bush meat has become a commercial industry. You see these guys [poachers] in refrigerated trucks and you know [that] it's not just for them."

Poaching for food is mainly a local affair. But poaching for animal parts isn't. It's a way to make money through the international market. Anyone who wants to can purchase practically any part of a giraffe just by doing an internet search. Giraffe skins (hides), bones, and tails fetch top dollar. A buyer can easily make online purchases through eBay or Amazon.com of all sorts of items made from real giraffe parts: jewelry, skins, carved bones, tails, rugs, pillows, and purses.

Giraffe parts are also sold for medicinal uses locally and internationally. Some cultures believe in the curative power of some animal body parts. Often the belief is tied to the animal's status as an endangered species—the fewer the animals in the wild, the more potent their magic or medicinal powers. In Tanzania, for example, human immunodeficiency virus and acquired immunodeficiency syndrome (HIV/AIDS) are widespread and considered an epidemic. Some Tanzanians believe that giraffe bone marrow and some parts of its head (usually the brain) can cure HIV/AIDS. Fresh giraffe heads and bones sell for about $140 each in Tanzania.

Giraffe hair and tails are also desired animal parts. For centuries the tail of a giraffe has been a symbol of authority in some parts of Africa. For example, chiefs of the Mondo tribe in the Democratic Republic of the Congo receive gifts of Kordofan giraffe tails to honor their position as head of the tribe. In some communities, a man gives a giraffe tail to the father of the woman he wishes to marry. More generally, the tail is used as a flyswatter to keep flying pests away. The long hair at the end of a giraffe tail is used to make jewelry, such as braided bracelets and necklaces. It may also be used as thread to create beaded jewelry and hair decorations. These items are sold locally and

HUMAN VIOLENCE AND CLIMATE CHANGE

around the world for as little as ten dollars apiece—and giraffe hair is not taken from live animals.

Poaching one kind of animal also feeds the poaching of other animals. In the Democratic Republic of the Congo and Tanzania, for example, poachers kill giraffes to feed the poachers who are tracking down elephants for ivory. "Giraffes are suffering as a result of . . . killing for ivory," says Julian Fennessy.

CHAD'S POACHING PROBLEM

Not all African countries have a poaching problem, but illegal killing of giraffes is a serious issue in Tanzania, Kenya, Chad, and the Democratic Republic of the Congo. The illegal activity in the central African nation of Chad is an example of the connection between poaching and military activity. Legally in Chad, giraffes are designated as a Category A species that benefits from full protection against any hunting. Yet most of central Africa, including Chad, has been impacted by decades of political strife and economic instability. The Zakouma National Park in southeastern Chad may be one of the last sanctuaries for wildlife in central Africa. The park provides a refuge for the largest surviving giraffe population in Chad.

Since 2003 the ongoing civil war between Sudan and South Sudan has been a humanitarian crisis. Hundreds of thousands of people in Darfur, a region in western Sudan, have been killed. Nearly two million Sudanese have been displaced, and three hundred thousand refugees found safety in Chad.

But Chad isn't immune from the conflict. In Chad, military groups, revolutionists, and terrorists smuggle many weapons. Weapons smuggling is big business worth millions of dollars. To buy weapons and other necessities of war, these militants poach wildlife to sell. Security in the region is weak, and if park guards get in the way of poachers, they are often murdered. Most poachers get away with their crimes.

The Kordofan giraffe *(G. c. antiquorum)* is native to Chad. At one time, large herds—as many as five to six thousand—roamed over a vast territory that spreads across Chad and the Central African Republic. Since the mid-1980s, the Kordofan giraffe's habitat has shrunk to Zakouma National Park, mainly due to illegal hunting and drought throughout the country. The giraffe population has remained steady within the park over the past two decades at nearly one thousand animals.

That number is small when compared to the thousands of giraffes that once roamed across Chad. The African Parks Network, a nongovernmental organization focused on conservation, is working with Chad's government to manage and protect critical conservation areas, including the Zakouma National Park. So the Kordofan's numbers are increasing.

LET'S TALK ABOUT TROPHY HUNTING

Big-game hunters track megafauna for sport. They typically hunt the Big Five animals, the ones that are most highly valued for their size, beauty, and the level of difficulty in finding and killing the animal. The Big Five are African lions, African elephants, African leopards, African white or black rhinos, and African buffalo. Africa is a top destination for big-game hunters.

For a long time, the animals were plentiful and hunting didn't impact their populations dramatically. Changes in the weapons of hunting changed the dynamics of killing. In ages past, a hunter would track and kill an animal for food and materials to survive. Humans had to get close enough to an animal to hit it with a spear or an arrow. The animal and its predator saw each other, eye to eye, most of the time. Hunting for food or for sport was a true human vs. animal match. With the invention of rifles and powerful scopes, the advantage shifted almost completely to human hunters. Finding the animal becomes the real part of the sport, because killing it is so easy. An animal seldom

A sports hunter in South Africa poses with his giraffe kill. Sports hunting is a lucrative business in Africa, although data about its economic impact is limited. By some estimates, trophy hunting brings in about $200 million every year. South Africa has the largest industry in terms of the number of hunters, animals killed, and income from sports hunting. Most of the hunting takes place on private reserves.

sees its killer, who can bring it down from a great distance and with great ease.

As the populations of the Big Five have dwindled—through habitat loss, poaching, and military conflicts—hunters face more of a challenge in finding the animals in the wild. Over the decades, the protected areas, where hunting is illegal, have increased. To meet the demand, some private businesses breed the animals in captivity and allow big-game hunters to stalk them on their land— for top dollar.

Most big-game hunters are trophy hunters, killing wild animals for their body parts to display. They do not hunt the animals for food.

Heads and hides are the most common trophy parts, though hunters also prize tusks, horns, and antlers. It is a lucrative business all over the world and especially in parts of Africa.

Trophy hunters kill an estimated 105,000 African animals each year. Supporters of the sport point to the fees hunters pay to hunt— sometimes well over $50,000 per trophy. They explain that the money goes toward conservation efforts in the country where the hunt takes place. Some African governments depend on that income as part of their economy.

In some African nations, including the Republic of South Africa, hunting giraffes is legal. South Africa has the largest hunting industry on the continent. For about $2,500 (trophy fee) and $1,000 per day for a guide, a hunter spends two or three days tracking a giraffe. After the kill, the hunter pays to have the giraffe's head and neck mounted as a trophy for display. The hunter may choose to keep the giraffe's hide as well. Rarely, a hunter exhibits the entire giraffe, either standing or sitting with its legs folded underneath. With the popularity of social media, hunters may kill the animal just to get a "kill shot," a photograph with the dead animal. Sometimes, after the photos are taken, the hunter gives the carcass to local residents for food, but the parts end up being sold on the international market.

WHAT IS THE UNITED STATES DOING?

Under the Endangered Species Act, a federal law since 1973, the US government plays a role in the survival of animals on its endangered species list. Two agencies administer this law: the Department of the Interior's US Fish and Wildlife Service (for land-based and freshwater wildlife) and the Commerce Department's US National Marine Fisheries Service (for oceanic wildlife). The Fish and Wildlife Service is responsible for dealing with the laws that restrict the types of animals allowed into the United States for retail sale, particularly if the animal is known to be endangered.

THE US ENDANGERED SPECIES ACT

The 1970s was a decade of intense environmental activism. In the United States, the work of conservationists, scientists, and journalists heightened public awareness of pollution and its impact on humans and wildlife. Rachel Carson's groundbreaking book *Silent Spring* in 1962 focused on the dangers of pesticides to birds, from songbirds like robins and blue jays to raptors like ospreys and eagles. Americans began to demand change.

The US government responded to the pressure from its citizens to protect ecosystems and species. The Environmental Protection Agency formed in 1970 to protect human health and the environment, and provide safe and clean air, water, and land for all Americans. In 1973 Congress passed the Endangered Species Act to establish and build a list of native animal species that were in danger of becoming extinct and to provide protections that would allow them to recover.

Enforced by the Fish and Wildlife Service and the National Marine Fisheries Service, the Endangered Species Act protects endangered species in three ways. First, all species on the act's endangered species list are protected from any activity that is authorized, funded, or carried out by the federal government if that activity harms the endangered animals or their habitat. Second, it is illegal for any person to "take" any group or individual on the protected list except with a federal permit, which is available only for conservation and scientific uses. The term *take* is defined as "to harass, harm, pursue, hunt, shoot, wound, kill, trap, capture, or collect or an attempt to engage in such conduct." Third, commerce of an endangered animal or its parts is considered a crime, and the penalties are fines from a few hundred to several thousand dollars.

The goal of the Endangered Species Act is not only to protect individual animals or plants but to bring a species back from the edge of extinction to full recovery and ongoing success of its population. The Fish and Wildlife Service and the National Marine Fisheries Service have biologists on staff who detail the steps needed to return a species to ecologically healthy numbers. Then the Fish and Wildlife Service works with other governmental agencies, nongovernmental organizations, experts, tribes, and others to carry out those plans. Once a species has recovered, it is removed from the list. In 2018 more than two thousand species of plants and animals were on the list. More than sixteen hundred of those live within US borders. For those creatures that are native to other parts of the world, the Endangered Species Act can't do much to protect their habitats or stop illegal hunting. However, the US government can and does place limits or outlaw the buying and selling of species on the CITES list and their parts.

The program works. Some animals in the United States that have been delisted, or removed from the endangered list, include the bald eagle (2007), the grizzly bear (2017), and the gray wolf (2017).

Because the giraffe is not yet on the endangered species list in the United States, the US government allows unlimited international trade of giraffe and giraffe parts into the country. The Fish and Wildlife Service and the Customs and Border patrol track the number of legally harvested giraffe trophies allowed into the United States. Between 2006 and 2015, nearly thirty-eight hundred giraffe trophies and more than thirty-five thousand other non-trophy giraffe pieces were legally imported into the United States. At a rate of more than three hundred items per year, the United States is a major importer of giraffe hunting trophies. In 2015, the most recent year for which data is available, the number grew to 457.

In April 2017, five organizations—including the Tucson, Arizona-based Center for Biological Diversity and the Washington, DC-based International Fund for Animal Welfare—submitted a petition to the US Department of the Interior and the Fish and Wildlife Service. The Center for Biological Diversity is a group of activists focused on fighting threats to the world's biodiversity. They use biological data, legal expertise, and petitions signed by citizens to bring about legislation that protects vulnerable wildlife and habitats. The International Fund for Animal Welfare, founded in 1969, provides leadership, innovation, and hands-on assistance to animals and communities around the world. The nonprofit group has offices in fifteen countries and projects in more than forty countries. The petition generated by these groups urged the US government to add giraffes to the list of protected animals under the Endangered Species Act. If the giraffe is added to the US endangered species list, importing giraffe parts would be limited or outlawed.

CLIMATE CHANGE = MORE DESERTS

Human activities such as deforestation and poaching harm wildlife directly. Naturally occurring events do too. One of the most devastating is drought, a period when an area receives below-average rainfall.

WHO'S WATCHING THE WORLD'S ANIMAL TRADE?

The Convention on International Trade in Endangered Species of Wild Fauna and Flora (CITES) is an international agreement among governments to monitor the trade of about thirty thousand plant species and fifty-eight hundred animal species. According to the CITES website, international wildlife trade is worth billions of dollars. It includes hundreds of millions of plant and animal specimens, both living and dead. The samples vary widely. A few examples include live fish or birds, food products, exotic leather goods, wooden musical instruments, timber, tourist collectibles, and medicines. The goal is to make sure international trade is not endangering the survival of these species.

The CITES agreement categorizes species across three lists, explained in three appendices:

APPENDIX I: includes species threatened with extinction. Trade is allowed only under extraordinary circumstances and never for commercial purposes. For example, a university may request a permit to import a species for a critical biological or botanical study.

APPENDIX II: includes species not threatened with extinction but control of trade for the species' survival is indicated

APPENDIX III: includes species that are protected in at least one country that has asked for help controlling the trade

So far, giraffes are not on any of the CITES lists. The Giraffe Conservation Foundation website explains that CITES doesn't recognize that there is any international trade in giraffes or their parts. Because of that, the species is not on their watch list. But at the World Wildlife Conference in Colombo, Sri Lanka, in 2019, a proposal was submitted to CITES for the inclusion of the giraffe *(G. c. camelopardalis)* in Appendix II.

Groups, including the Giraffe Conservation Foundation, will continue to keep an eye on giraffe trade and investigate situations as warranted. They're especially watching the countries in East Africa and central Africa, where this trade appears to be increasing.

Human interference, such as overuse of water resources, can also cause drought.

Giraffes depend on the moisture content from the leaves they eat for the water they need. They can get by for days without drinking water from a large body such as a river or lake. In some areas, such as northwestern Namibia, giraffes have even become water independent and don't need to drink water at all.

Giraffes browse a variety of plants, although most of their diet—about 75 percent—is dependent on just a few specific plants. During the wet season, a period of months when rainfall is regular and plentiful, giraffes munch on a wider variety of foods: fruit, leaves, and twigs. The number one choice among giraffes? The leaves of the acacia tree. The tree's thick leaves provide plenty of water for the giraffes.

DID YOU KNOW?

GIRAFFES WILL DRINK WATER IF IT'S AVAILABLE. THEY HAVE TO SPLAY THEIR FRONT LEGS TO GET LOW ENOUGH TO DRINK, WHICH MAKES THEM VULNERABLE TO PREDATORS. HOWEVER, MOST GIRAFFES LIVE IN ARID REGIONS WITH FEW WATERING HOLES. THEY DEPEND ON THE FOG THAT COMES IN FROM THE COAST AND LANDS AS DROPLETS OF WATER ON LEAVES DURING THE NIGHT AND MORNING HOURS.

A baby giraffe drinks from a waterhole in Etosha National Park in Namibia. The long-legged animal splays its legs to lower itself to the water. Prolonged drought as a result of climate change endangers giraffe survival.

HUMAN VIOLENCE AND CLIMATE CHANGE

THE SAHARA SHIFT

From fossil evidence, scientists know that at one time giraffes lived in the driest area of Africa—the Sahara. This desert region hasn't always existed as a sand-covered wasteland. Slight wobbles in Earth's axis have caused periods of both humidity, or rainfall, and aridity, or dryness, in this region. About eleven thousand years ago, the Sahara began being drenched with rainfall from seasonal monsoons. Those heavy rains produced lakes, rivers, grasslands, and even some forests, creating a lush landscape.

Large animals moved to the lush area. Fossil remains and rock carvings prove that elephants, rhinos, hippos, crocodiles, and giraffes lived in the Sahara region during this time. "The climate change which turned most of the . . . Sahara into a savannah-style environment happened within a few hundred years only," says Stefan Kroepelin of the University of Cologne in Germany. But the humid period did not last. Between eight thousand and forty-five hundred years ago, the Saharan terrain experienced another shift to a dry period and rapidly returned to its previous desert conditions. The people and animals that had lived there moved to other parts of Africa where they could find food and water to survive. These drought conditions persist.

Partly because of climate change, the Sahara is growing—it is 10 percent larger than it was one hundred years ago. Although the desert's boundaries normally increase and decrease during the dry and wet seasons, experts have documented a wider expansion of the desert during the twentieth and early twenty-first centuries. As the arid region expands, plants and wildlife die out or move to greener areas for survival.

THE SAHARA SHIFT: THEN vs. NOW

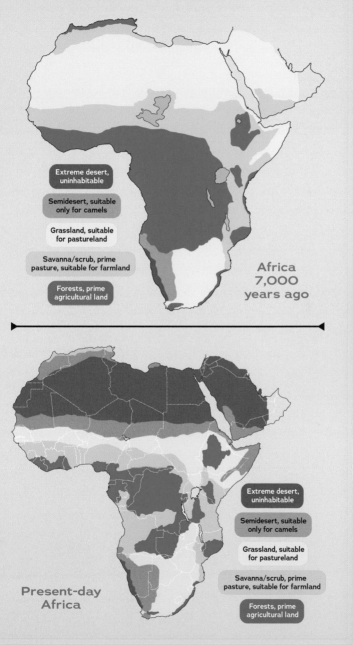

Extreme desert,
uninhabitable

Semidesert, suitable
only for camels

Grassland, suitable
for pastureland

Savanna/scrub, prime
pasture, suitable for farmland

Forests, prime
agricultural land

Africa
7,000
years ago

Extreme desert,
uninhabitable

Semidesert, suitable
only for camels

Grassland, suitable
for pastureland

Savanna/scrub, prime
pasture, suitable for farmland

Forests, prime
agricultural land

Present-day
Africa

During dry seasons, acacia trees become the mainstay of their diets, because many remain green even after the rains are long gone. Loss of vegetation in giraffe country is a growing problem in many parts of Africa because it leaves giraffes without the trees they need for food and water.

Drought happens naturally and often in cycles, but climate change is expanding the amount of fertile land that is vulnerable to drought. And the droughts are lasting longer and are more severe. Many acres of fertile land are drying up permanently and degrading into deserts. Scientists call this desertification. Experts estimate that nearly 30 million acres (12 million ha) of farmable land worldwide is lost each year to desertification.

The nations of Africa have been especially challenged. About 80 percent of the continent's overall economy depends on subsistence farming, or raising just enough livestock and growing just enough crops to feed one's family. Loss of this land through drought or warfare can mean starvation to families. So they move into areas where the land is still fertile—where wildlife also lives. As families cut down trees and remove native plants to build homes and farms, they reduce the amount of habitat for wildlife. The removal of this flora adds to the process of desertification.

As the ground dries up because of desertification and drought, plant life dries up and withers, becoming extremely vulnerable to fire. In dry landscapes, a single lightning strike or human carelessness, such as neglecting a campfire, dropping a lit match, or causing a spark, can easily ignite widespread and damaging fires. Few natural phenomena are as destructive as brush fires. They begin in dry areas and quickly spread to more fertile areas where they destroy healthy plants and trees—and the wildlife that lives there. Giraffes can sometimes escape fires and suffer little to no injury. However, the trees and bushes they depend on for food and water can disappear in a matter of hours or days. Recovery of those plants can take many years, if they recover at all.

IT ALL ADDS UP

Sometimes a species can disappear forever because of a single event or cause: a deadly disease, overhunting, destruction of habitat, or widespread fires. For giraffes, the causes of their decline are numerous, varied, and often difficult to reverse.

"Only recently have we looked at them critically and seen this huge drop, which has been a shock to the conservation community." says Jeff Flocken, the former regional director of the International Fund for Animal Welfare. "This is an iconic animal and it's in deep trouble."

Conservation of natural resources works hand-in-hand with conservation of animal species. Experts in Africa—with support from many others around the world—are busy analyzing the problems and coming up with amazing solutions. And the news isn't all bad.

CHAPTER 6

THE GOOD NEWS OF GIRAFFE CONSERVATION

The greatest threats to any environment and animal species come from two main sources: nature itself and human activities. But humans can also create positive change. Human helpers are the frontline forces working to save giraffes. They are making a difference.

Conservationists work to preserve, protect, and restore these critical elements of our planet:

- the environment in general
- ecosystems (rain forests, coral reefs, savannas, oceans, and other natural areas)
- flora (plant life)
- fauna (animal life)
- natural resources (minerals and water)

Conservation is based on scientific principles and uses evidence-based methods to record, analyze, and make plans

Julian Fennessy (*left*) cofounded the Giraffe Conservation Foundation with his wife, Stephanie (*right*). Working with a ranger (*center*), the Fennessys capture a Nubian giraffe in Uganda's Murchison Falls National Park as part of a translocation project.

for improvement. That takes a team. Conservation of species reached a turning point in 1978. That year world leaders in conservation biology—scientists, wildlife conservationists, and zookeepers—met in San Diego, California, to discuss the alarming rise in animal extinction rates. They agreed that it was time for all the experts to share the information they were gathering and work together to save the endangered and threatened creatures on our planet.

In the twenty-first century, highly trained experts and innumerable workers and volunteers continue to work toward the goal of saving at-risk species. They are passionate people who believe it is the duty of human beings to manage and preserve the environment for future generations. The people who are working to save giraffes have made it their life's mission to study, learn, and share their findings so that this species survives. It takes hard work and a lot of money.

79

THE GIRAFFE CONSERVATION FOUNDATION

Julian and Stephanie Fennessy are passionate about giraffes. Dedicating their lives to helping these creatures, the couple cofounded the Giraffe Conservation Foundation. He earned a PhD in biological science from the University of Sydney in Australia, and she has an MS degree in environmental engineering and sustainable infrastructure. They moved from Australia to Namibia in southwestern Africa to build and direct the foundation.

The foundation describes itself as the only nongovernmental organization in the world to focus exclusively on the conservation and management of giraffes in the wild throughout Africa. The group works with partners in Africa and around the world to explore and put into practice ways to sustain and conserve the lives of giraffes in the wild. The foundation works closely with IUCN Species Survival Commission Giraffe and Okapi Specialist Group. Julian Fennessy is cochair of the group, and Stephanie Fennessy is the secretary. The foundation works hard to make sure the rest of the world knows what's happening with giraffes in Africa. The foundation extended its reach beyond the borders of Africa by creating two international branches, one in the United States and one in Germany.

The foundation and its partners raise money for their projects from sources all over the world. Some of this income is in grants, but most of their funding comes from foundations, zoos, and individuals who give money to support its work. Most of the donations come from the United States. Most of that money, 91 percent, goes directly toward giraffe conservation and management. The rest covers staffing and administration costs.

One of its newest programs gives people an easy way to donate. "Adopt a Giraffe" is popular with families and children because they feel connected to a specific giraffe they have "adopted." The adoption fee goes toward the conservation work the foundation does, and the donor receives a packet of giraffe-related items. The website shows the names, photos, and descriptions of six "adoptable" giraffes at https://giraffeconservation.org/adopt-a-giraffe/.

Giraffe conservation is difficult because of the variety and complexity of problems the animal faces across a very large continent. Methods of conservation that are absolutely essential in one place may be unnecessary in another. In Niger, for example, people and giraffes share a common area and coexist in relative peace. In other regions, however, people see giraffes as a threat to their livelihood. Conservation organizations have established educational programs for the people in those areas, and so fewer giraffes are killed. Sometimes giraffes need to be moved to improve their chances for survival and increase their populations.

Researchers have found that giraffes living in protected areas, such as reserves or national parks, are actually not doing as well as hoped. Instead, the real progress has been happening in private and community-based sanctuaries. There, partnerships between conservation organizations and private tourism groups come up with solutions that benefit everyone. And in these places, the giraffe population is holding steady or even increasing.

STANDING TALL FOR THE GIRAFFE

The Giraffe Conservation Foundation has been working with other groups that form the IUCN Species Survival Commission Giraffe and Okapi Specialist Group. The foundation has been vital to the work on behalf of the giraffe in Africa—publicizing concerns, coming up with plans, and carrying them out. Julian Fennessy, leader of both groups, headed a large project to research and deliver the first-ever detailed status report on giraffe conservation across Africa. With this information, the Giraffe Conservation Foundation and other conservation groups can develop action plans to help giraffes and measure the plans' ongoing success.

It takes a network of groups to save giraffes. Together, African governments, nongovernmental organizations such as the Giraffe Conservation Foundation, colleges and universities, independent researchers, and international organizations coordinate efforts, share information, and develop programs to improve the giraffe's chances of survival. These groups also work to improve the lives of the people who live among giraffes. These animals are a keystone species in Africa, attracting tourists, photographers, and nature enthusiasts from around the world. These visitors bring much-needed money to the countries, many of them poor, where giraffes can still be seen in the wild.

Because each country has a different set of problems and possibilities, many kinds of conservation programs are underway across Africa. Some focus on a particular giraffe subspecies. Others help subspecies in several regions. A number of projects across giraffe country are doing remarkable work for the sake of giraffe survival.

SPOTLIGHT: THE ASSOCIATION TO SAFEGUARD THE GIRAFFES OF NIGER

In the West African country of Niger, several devastating events over the last half of the twentieth century brought the West African giraffe within a neck's width of extinction. These events included significant loss of habitat, poaching, military activity, and drought. In 1996 the population of the subspecies was a scant forty-nine animals. Without immediate intervention, they were likely to become extinct within a few years. So the IUCN upgraded their status from Vulnerable to Endangered.

Isabelle Ciofolo, an ethologist—someone who studies animal behavior—was the first person to study giraffes in Niger. She founded the Association for Saving the Giraffes of Niger. Armed with critical information from Ciofolo and other experts, Niger's government got involved. Officials started enforcing a decade-old law against poaching, and incidents of illegal hunting fell dramatically. Working with Ciofolo's association, the government also set up educational and public awareness programs for the local people to learn more about giraffes and the threats they face.

Giraffes are protected in Niger's giraffe zone to the east of the nation's capital city of Niamey. Once widespread throughout West Africa, West African giraffes (*Giraffa camelopardalis peralta*) such as this one live only in Niger, where they are protected from poaching and other threats. Once down to only forty-nine animals in the wild, the giraffe population in Niger has rebounded through conservation efforts to more than six hundred.

• •

The association has been a critical part of the conservation strategy in Niger. The group has taken part in annual census counts of giraffes. They have worked with locals to protect giraffe habitat. They have bolstered local economies so people do not have to turn to poaching to earn money. For example, the association has provided small interest-free microloans to women to help them set up small businesses. Workers with the association have helped local farmers dig water holes, set up grain mills and cereal banks (for storing ground grains), and provided seeds and fertilizer. In exchange, the association asks local peoples to find ways to coexist with the giraffes rather than destroying habitat by expanding croplands.

A road sign about an hour outside of the protected giraffe zone in Niamey, Niger, alerts drivers to be on the lookout for giraffes.

To better protect giraffes, the Niger government established a giraffe zone not far from Niger's capital city of Niamey. All poaching is prohibited there, and officials keep a close eye on any activity. Local people earn money by selling snacks, artwork, leather goods, and needlework to tourists who come to see giraffes in the zone. Because of these efforts, locals see the giraffe as a positive part of their environment rather than as competitors for land.

Like most nongovernmental organizations, the association depends on funds from international groups and projects. The African Wildlife Foundation partners with them on many of their conservation efforts. It's paying off. Conservation efforts on behalf of the West African giraffe is one of Africa's greatest successes. The most recent census in 2016 counted about six hundred West African giraffes. In November 2018, the West African giraffe's IUCN Red List status was moved from Endangered back to Vulnerable.

The number is still too low to expect the giraffe population to recover without continuing the efforts. The Giraffe Conservation Foundation and the Sahara Conservation Fund are creating a second giraffe zone. They plan to move several giraffes from the giraffe zone of the Kouré Reserve, about 37 miles (60 km) southeast of Niamey, to the Gadabeji Game Reserve in central Niger, where the West African giraffe once lived. Both groups will monitor the giraffes' progress in this protected zone.

SPOTLIGHT: THE RETICULATED GIRAFFE PROJECT IN KENYA

The Reticulated Giraffe Project is based in the Samburu National Reserve in Kenya. It focuses its work on several research projects to save the current population of reticulated giraffes and to turn the corner toward increasing their numbers. The IUCN Red List status for the reticulated giraffe is Endangered. Project partners include organizations all over the world from zoos and private foundations to experts such as Anne Innis Dagg.

The project's coordinator is John Doherty, who started studying giraffes when he was ten years old and living in Kenya. The project's

Reticulated giraffes (*Giraffa reticulata*) browse in Samburu National Reserve in Kenya.

mission is to work with a network of people and groups to stop and reverse the decline in the giraffe's populations. This network shares information, experience, effort, and expertise.

Doherty says, "I think the situation is quite serious. The first three years I was working in Kenya, there was no rain at all. It just didn't rain. People were starving and coped by eating anything they could find, including giraffe. And it dawned on me that we were actually witnessing a megafaunal extinction happening right now, not seen on this scale since the disappearance of the woolly mammoth at the end of the last ice age."

The project staff is working with local villagers who live on the eastern border of the reserve, an area impacted by the war in neighboring Somalia. The project is also working with camel herders in the northern desert area of the reserve, with children in Kenya's capital of Nairobi, and with tribal elders who value the giraffe and remember a time when many more roamed their world. One of Doherty's unique ideas is having local people choose a particular giraffe in the reserve and name it after one of their relatives. Then, when they recognized "their" giraffe in the wild, they felt a connection with it.

The survival of giraffes depends to a great degree on the communities that share their space with them. So staff members also have joined with the BOMA Project, creating a team of twenty-eight village mentors and three field officers. A *boma* is an East African livestock enclosure used by herders. It is a symbol of sanctuary and protection. The team keeps an eye on and collects data about the reticulated giraffes that live outside of protected areas.

SPOTLIGHT: ROTHSCHILD'S GIRAFFE PROJECT IN KENYA AND UGANDA

Many African countries are home to only one subspecies of giraffe. Kenya is home to three: the reticulated, the Masai, and the Rothschild's giraffe. In fact, some of the oldest giraffe fossils have been found in

A Rothschild's Giraffe Project team moved giraffes in an adapted barge across Lake Baringo in Kenya to a conservancy area on the other side.

• •

Kenya. Some scientists think that the entire species of giraffe may have originated in Kenya, spreading out from there over the centuries. The original territory of Rothschild's giraffes was on the shores of Kenya's Lake Baringo. They were once known as Baringo giraffes. Beyond Kenya, a few pockets of Rothschild's giraffes also live in Uganda. Their total population in 2016 was 1,671 (up from 670 in a 2010 census).

Established in 2009, the Rothschild's Giraffe Project is the main project of the Giraffe Research and Conservation Trust organization, headquartered in Nairobi, Kenya. It is the only research project devoted just to learning more about the Rothschild's giraffe and to developing a strategy for their survival.

One strategic move toward that goal happened in February 2011. Zoe Muller, coordinator of the project, worked with the Giraffe Conservation Foundation to launch an unheard-of project. The members of the project figured out how to move eight giraffes from the Soysambu Conservancy in west-central Kenya to the Lake Baringo area

THE GOOD NEWS OF GIRAFFE CONSERVATION

of Kenya where Rothschild's giraffes lived more than forty years ago. Loss of habitat forced the giraffes out of the area, and none have been seen there since. Because of the establishment of the community-led Ruko Conservancy in that area, it was safe for the Rothschild's giraffes to return and start a new population. The trick was to find a way to move them. No roads exist in that part of Kenya, so moving them by truck was not possible. The team members realized they would have to move the giraffes across Lake Baringo—and giraffes can't swim.

Muller explains the challenge: "Giraffes may look laid-back, but ask them to do anything more than eat leaves and lope around the savanna and they tend to get very stressed, so we knew we had to [organize] the translocation with forethought and care. After four years of planning we were ready. The operation would be carried out in stages to [minimize] trauma to the animals and increase our chances of success."

The team selected eight giraffes from the Soysambu Conservancy to make the move. It took three days to catch them. After giving them three weeks to recover from the stress of their capture, the team began the move toward the lake. They loaded the giraffes onto a large, specially built truck late at night. After a long, slow, bumpy ride, they arrived at the shore of Lake Baringo. The next step was to get across the body of water—5 miles (8 km) wide—in two trips, four giraffes at a time.

The team had built a makeshift boat for the giraffes. They attached canoes to the sides of a barge that had been altered to create a holding area for four giraffes. The animals walked calmly onto the barge and looked around, their heads sticking out over the canvas sides of the holding area, as they took the one-hour voyage to the other side of the lake. When they arrived, they ambled off the boat, down a ready-made walled ramp, and back onto land. Muller describes the release: "As soon as the doors to the holding area were opened there was a clatter of hooves and all four giraffes burst off the barge and galloped up the chute to freedom—and an enormous cheer from the crowd that had gathered. The second batch fared much the same: the animals stood quietly during the smooth crossing, then rushed up the chute in an explosion of muscle and long legs."

The eight giraffes remain healthy, roaming freely across the conservancy land. Muller and her colleagues hope that their numbers will grow and that the Rothschild's giraffes at Lake Baringo will make a comeback.

SPOTLIGHT: OPERATION TWIGA, TWIGA II, AND TWIGA III IN UGANDA

The first ever World Giraffe Day, launched by the Giraffe Conservation Foundation, occurred on June 21, 2015. The goal of the day was to raise enough money to move eighteen Rothschild's giraffes from the northern part of Murchison Falls National Park in Uganda to the southern part. The challenge? The Nile River runs through the park, so the conservation teams needed help to get the giraffes across the river.

The Giraffe Conservation Foundation, Uganda Wildlife Authority, Uganda Wildlife Education Centre, and many other groups wanted to make the move to increase the giraffes' range in the park. By giving the giraffes a bigger territory for browsing and for finding mates, the groups hope this endangered subspecies will have a better chance to survive.

And the northern side of the park is more developed than it once was. According to Patrick Atimnedi, Uganda Wildlife Authority's manager of veterinary services,

> The range of development projects in the northern sector has the potential to impact negatively on the giraffe stock. As this Park is separated by the Nile, and giraffe, unlike other animals like elephant, cannot swim across the river, they are concentrated in the northern sector; that is why we have to help them cross that natural barrier.

Encouraged by the success of the Lake Baringo translocation, the team captured eighteen giraffes for the Murchison project, which they dubbed Twiga, a Swahili word for "giraffe." They attached GPS satellite collars to five of the giraffes. Over three weeks in early 2016, they moved all eighteen giraffes across the river, in three groups of six. Team members used the same techniques as the Kenyan translocation. The only difference was that they ferried an entire truck carrying the giraffes across the river rather than off-loading the animals from a truck onto a barge. One less step meant less stress for the movable beasts.

The following year, World Giraffe Day raised enough money to move more giraffes across the river in the park. Operation Twiga II repeated the success, adding nineteen giraffes to the translocated population. This time, the team took the first-ever X-rays of giraffe feet in the wild. They hope what they learn from studying these X-rays will help zoos around the world better understand and treat hoof issues in their giraffes.

Next up? Twiga III, which will be funded by World Giraffe Day 2018 donations, to move more giraffes in the park. Each year World Giraffe Day celebrates the world's longest-necked animal on the longest day (or night) of the year, June 21. Check out the website to learn more about World Giraffe Day at https://giraffeconservation.org/world -giraffe-day/.

SPOTLIGHT: PROJECT GIRAFFE IN TANZANIA

Among giraffes, the largest subspecies population is the Masai giraffe, with about thirty-seven thousand animals. They live in central and southern Kenya and in Tanzania, and some have been translocated to Rwanda. Tanzania has designated the giraffe as its national animal because more giraffes live in Tanzania than in any other country in the world. But those numbers are falling.

The Masai giraffes are being squeezed out of their territories by dramatic increases in human populations, especially in areas surrounding the Masai Mara National Reserve. As with other giraffe subspecies, the Masai giraffes are also victims of poaching, mainly for bushmeat.

The US-based Wild Nature Institute has launched Project GIRAFFE (GIRAffe Facing Fragmentation Effects) to help the Masai giraffes. The focus is to gather as much demographic data as possible about births, deaths, and movement as well as the effects of natural and human factors on the giraffe populations. Project GIRAFFE scientists begin by studying the giraffe populations. Then they look closely at the effects of habitat fragmentation. They monitor giraffe birth rates, survival rates, and movements across territory to evaluate the increase or decrease of the population. Derek Lee of Dartmouth College in New Hampshire has been working with the institute since 2011. The information he and his colleagues gather is shared among wildlife organizations to come up with solutions to help these giraffes.

Like other conservation groups, the institute also believes that education is a key to helping wildlife survive. So the institute and its partners create and distribute a variety of materials—books, posters, lesson plans, and workshops—to teachers and children throughout Tanzania. Video books via smartphones have reached even remote villages. For adults, the institute supports village-based community environmental forums, where local residents can interact with wildlife experts. They discuss many natural resource issues, including improved land use, solutions to drought, human-wildlife competition, and more.

SPOTLIGHT: SNARES TO WARES IN UGANDA

One of the most unique projects in eastern Africa is a joint effort between Michigan State University and the Uganda Wildlife

The Crafts Boys of Pakwach, a town in northern Uganda, convert illegal wire snares into items to sell in the market. The Snares to Wares project is a collaboration between Michigan State University researchers and the Uganda Wildlife Authority.

Authority. It's known as Snares to Wares. Poachers in Uganda's Murchison Falls National Park set illegal wildlife traps called snares, made of wire from old tires. To get the wires that are embedded in tires, poachers burn off a tire's rubber. They shape the wires into nooses and attach them to trunks and branches of trees and bushes in the park. As wildlife moves through the vegetation, their necks, legs, or feet get caught in the sharp wire traps. Poachers come through the area looking for trapped animals. When they find them, they finish the job, killing lions, elephants, giraffes, and other animals, which they use and sell mostly for food. Animals that escape the snares are often maimed, losing a foot or leg. Others become ill or die from wound infections.

Robert Montgomery of Michigan State University runs the Research on the Ecology of Carnivores and their Prey. He works with East African students to develop innovative conservation projects in their homeland. Out of this lab came the idea for Snares to Wares.

"Removing snares from the landscape is critically important to the survival of some of the most enigmatic and important wildlife on our planet," explains Montgomery. But removing the snares isn't enough. It's difficult to dispose of piles and piles of wire—and easy for poachers to steal back what's been recovered from the bush. To solve this, something needed to be done with the wire.

Along with graduate student Tutilo Mudumba, Montgomery came up with a plan: shape the wires into toys and works of art that can be sold at the park in Uganda, online at the Snares to Wares website, and elsewhere—including Michigan. One of the poorest villages in Uganda, Pakwach, is near the Murchison Falls National Park and was a good place to start. "There are youth in Pakwach, ages 11 to 12, who [do not attend] secondary school and have little to do. As they get older, they become potential recruits for poachers," Montgomery says. "We are teaching the young men how to form the wires into sculptures of the animals that are being snared," he continues, "so people locally and globally can truly help conserve wildlife. We cannot address the problem of snaring without addressing the livelihood issues. . . . We think this project will help do both."

AND THE LIST GOES ON

Many other projects, programs, and people are also actively working on ways to ensure that giraffes do not become extinct. Experts, villagers, and supporters around the world are sticking their necks out for giraffes in ingenious ways. You can join in on the efforts too!

CHAPTER 7

SPEAKING UP FOR GIRAFFES

The time to speak up is now. Wildlife experts have done the work, exposed the problems, and sounded the call to action. It takes a global community to make a difference, and that community includes people like you. Giraffes can't speak for themselves, so let's figure out how we can all break the silence and get the word out.

SOCIAL MEDIA AND CITIZEN SCIENCE

Few activities in history have been as effective as social media for moving people to take up a cause and share information. Social media can do good things. Whether you're on Snapchat, Instagram, or any other online platform, including your own blog or website or YouTube channel, you can become an influencer. Your words have the power to shape the discussions, directions, and behavior of those who pay attention to what you share. You have the power to share the story of giraffes' impending extinction. If you want to become a source of positive change for giraffe conservation, here are some ways to get started:

You can help giraffes in a variety of ways. Start by visiting your local zoo to learn more about the animals. Talk to the volunteer coordinator to learn about volunteer opportunities. Share what you are learning with your social media community.

1. Follow some of the giraffe conservation groups or individuals mentioned in this book. Find them at their websites and on social media—usually Facebook, Instagram, and Twitter. Sign up for their online newsletters. Share what you are learning on your social media pages.

2. When you post about giraffe conservation, use hashtags to make searches easy and to build interest in the topic. Encourage your friends to share the information you post using the same hashtags. Here are some examples: #giraffeconservation, #silentextinction, #savethegiraffes, #giraffesforever.

3. Create a Pinterest board about giraffes. Pin photos, news stories, conservation updates, graphics, and basic giraffe facts. Invite your friends to follow your board.

4. Retweet, retweet, retweet. Once you follow a giraffe organization or you see an article about giraffes on Twitter, love the tweet and share it. Get your followers to retweet to build the audience and spread the message. Comment on the Tweet to encourage the person who posted the tweet to continue sharing what they know.

5. Start a blog. You can write about giraffes in general, the problems they're facing, good news from conservation groups, and anything else related to wildlife issues.

6. Take photos or record videos of the giraffes at your local zoo and upload them on social media, using hashtags. Provide information about the subspecies, the zoos, and other material to educate your audience.

7. Get involved in conservation programs as a citizen scientist. Sometimes you can assist these efforts just by getting on the internet, as with the San Diego Zoo's Wildwatch Kenya program. Hundreds of thousands of helpers use Zooniverse, where they log in to aid researchers with different kinds of animal conservation projects.

SCHOOL PROJECTS

Every year students have to come up with topics for reports and projects. Whether you are writing for science class, English, or social studies, giraffes in the wild are a great topic to choose. Use a variety of information from books and websites to present the most recent news about the status of giraffes and about conservation work in Africa. You might even be able to interview someone at your local zoo to add more detail.

Don't be afraid to use the Contact Us forms on websites to do some of the research and to ask questions. People involved in giraffe conservation are warm, friendly, smart, and very happy to share what they know. They get excited knowing others are speaking up for the giraffe!

NEWS

As a citizen in your community, you have the right to contact communication organizations about things that matter to you. From newspapers to radio shows to television news, you can suggest stories or write opinion pieces about the silent extinction facing giraffes. You might be surprised to find that media outlets are eager to find out more about topics like this because they know other viewers and readers will be interested too. To figure out who to contact about a story idea, check out the websites of the media outlets that interest you most in your town. The sites will tell you where to email your idea and how to present it. The same is true for submitting an opinion piece. Check out the website of the news organization to which you want to write and look for the Opinion or Letters to the Editor tab. There you'll learn more about where to email your letter and how to craft it for submission.

ZOOS

If your local zoo has a giraffe—or two or three—visit and find out what conservation programs the zoo supports. Most zoos celebrate World Giraffe Day on June 21 with special events, and it can be fun to take part in that day. If your zoo doesn't celebrate the event, suggest it to them.

Many zoos offer summer internships for high school and college students to help with animals, including giraffes. Many zoos also need volunteers, from young people to seniors. Check the zoo's website for more information about qualifications and how to get involved.

FUND-RAISERS

Many organizations make it possible for people to donate to their causes, and giraffe conservation groups are no different. Most of them are legitimate, but do your research. Read reviews about the organization, and use your best judgment before making a donation. Ask a trusted adult for their input too.

MARK YOUR CALENDAR: JUNE 21 IS WORLD GIRAFFE DAY

What can you celebrate on the longest day of the year (or night, depending on where you live)? The animal with the world's longest neck—the giraffe! The Giraffe Conservation Foundation launched World Giraffe Day in 2014 to celebrate the amazing giraffe and to raise money, create awareness, and educate people about the plight of giraffes in the wild. Zoos, schools, companies, conservation organizations, governments, and other groups host the annual event.

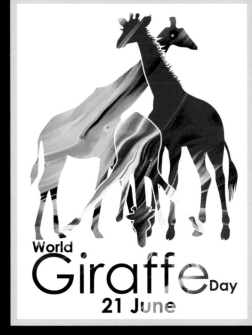

Each year a specific giraffe conservation program is the focus of World Giraffe Day, and the donations from it go directly to that cause. In a few years, the day has grown into a powerful way to spread the news about giraffes and to raise money for conservation. Find out more about past efforts and upcoming events at https://giraffeconservation.org/world-giraffe-day/. Think about working with your friends to host a fund-raiser at your school, or volunteer if your local zoo is planning activities for the next World Giraffe Day.

Some organizations offer matching dollars during special fund-raising events. Then a big donor matches the amount of money that smaller donors raise, doubling the impact of the giving. If you sign up for newsletters or follow groups online, you will find out about other opportunities for giving.

You can also start your own fund-raiser to collect money for giraffe conservation. Choose a specific project to support. Then contact the people who run the project to find out if they are interested in your fund-raising efforts. They may have press kits ready for you to use that include logos, photos, and other helpful promotional material. Then decide how you're going to raise the money: by taking direct donations in person or by selling braided bracelets or other handmade goods at your school. Make sure you get permission, and follow any guidelines from your school or local community. You can also use already-established fund-raising programs to sell candy bars, magazines, cookies, popcorn, or other items and designate the money you earn for your chosen giraffe project.

MORE THAN AN ICON

Giraffes need us all to care about and protect them for their long-term survival. The people who have and are working on their behalf in Africa devote their lives to making sure this beautiful, gentle giant never becomes a mere icon. From the beginning, *Giraffa camelopardalis* has walked a long, hard road. Let's make sure that giraffes continue to cast their long shadows under the bright African sun.

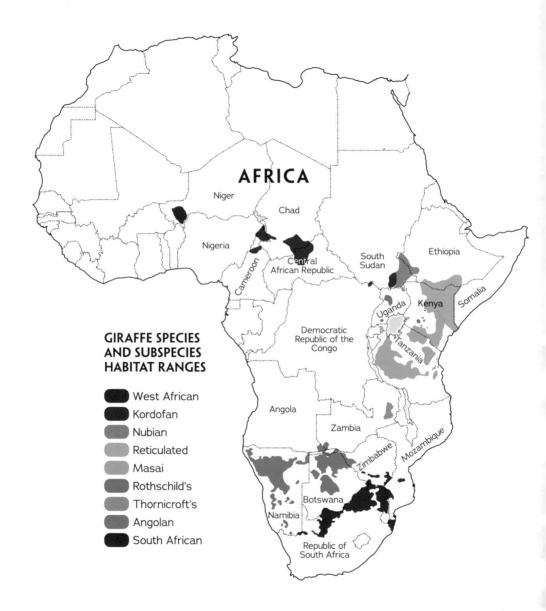

AFRICA

Niger

Chad

Nigeria

Cameroon

Central African Republic

South Sudan

Ethiopia

Uganda

Kenya

Somalia

Democratic Republic of the Congo

Tanzania

Angola

Zambia

Mozambique

Zimbabwe

Botswana

Namibia

Republic of South Africa

GIRAFFE SPECIES AND SUBSPECIES HABITAT RANGES

- West African
- Kordofan
- Nubian
- Reticulated
- Masai
- Rothschild's
- Thornicroft's
- Angolan
- South African

This color-coded map shows where the nine giraffe subspecies live in Africa.

GIRAFFE GUIDE

This introduction to each of the nine subspecies of giraffes, including status, is based on the IUCN Red List. The overall status for the species *Giraffa camelopardalis* is Vulnerable. In some cases, scientists have determined that a subspecies is Endangered. Population data is from 2015 and 2016, the most recent years for which statistical information is available. Each subspecies' Red List status was updated in 2018.

   The focus for conservationists is the actual number of individual giraffes for each subspecies. Even if a group of giraffes with a low population count is increasing in numbers, it would take only one event—a drought or disease or war—to completely eliminate that subspecies. While it is good news when a subspecies is growing in numbers, that is not enough to change its status or stop working to protect these animals.

REGION: WEST AFRICA

Subspecies: West African giraffe *(G. c. peralta)*

Where they are found: only in or near the giraffe zone, a protected area in Niger

Coat color and pattern: tan-colored, slightly rectangular spots. Its cream-colored lines are wide. Overall, this giraffe is light in color. Its spots continue partway down the legs, ending at the knee and hock (the knee part that bends backward on the back legs). Lower legs are white with no patterns.

Ossicones: They sit far apart and stand straight up like antennae. Males have a prominent median, or center, ossicone.

Population in 1990s: 50
Population in 2015: 400
Status: Increasing
Red List status: Vulnerable
Population in zoos worldwide: 0

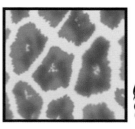

REGION: CENTRAL AFRICA

Subspecies: Kordofan giraffe (*G. c. antiquorum*)

Where they are found: savannas of Cameroon, Central African Republic, Chad (Zakouma National Park), Democratic Republic of the Congo (Garamba National Park), and South Sudan

Coat color and pattern: pale with irregular shapes, surrounded by whitish outlines. The pattern also appears on the inner legs.

Ossicones: two main ossicones. Males have a median ossicone.

Population in 1980s: 3,696

Population in 2016: 2,000

Status: Decreasing

Red List status: Critically Endangered

Population in zoos worldwide: 65

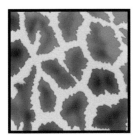

REGION: EASTERN AFRICA

Subspecies: Nubian giraffe *(G. c. camelopardalis)*

Where they are found: savannas and woodlands of Ethiopia and South Sudan and in isolated areas of Uganda and Kenya

Coat color and pattern: chestnut brown, well-defined (usually four-sided) spots cover the body and head. Its belly has no spots. Those on the legs stop at the knee. The lower legs are white with no patterns.

Ossicones: two main ossicones. Males have one median ossicone.

Population in 1980s: 20,577
Population in 2016: 650
Status: Decreasing
Red List status: Critically Endangered
Population in zoos worldwide: Unknown

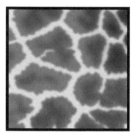

Subspecies: Reticulated Giraffe *(G. c. reticulata)*
Where they are found: savannas, woodlands, flood plains, and rain forests of Kenya, Somalia, and Ethiopia

Coat color and pattern: large reddish-brown spots with clear edges. Thick white spaces separate the spots and give the pattern a reticulated, or netlike, look. The pattern continues down the legs, fading slightly before reaching the feet.

Ossicones: two main ossicones. Males have one median ossicone.

Population in 1990s: 36,000 to 47,750
Population in 2016: 8,661
Status: Decreasing
Red List status: Endangered
Population in zoos worldwide: 450

Subspecies: Masai Giraffe *(G. c. tippelskirchi)*
Where they are found: savannas of Kenya and Tanzania

Coat color and pattern: Of the nine subspecies, the Masai giraffe may be the easiest to identify. Its spots are much darker than those of other giraffes, and they tend to be star-shaped, with jagged edges. The spotting goes all the way down the legs to the hooves.

Ossicones: two main ossicones. Males usually have one median ossicone but not always.

Population in 1970s: 66,449
Population in 2016: 31,611
Status: Decreasing
Red List status: Vulnerable
Population in zoos worldwide: 100

Subspecies: Rothschild's Giraffe *(G. c. rothschildi)*
Where they are found: savannas of Kenya and Uganda

Coat color and pattern: cream-colored spaces frame light- to medium-brown patches. The lower legs do not have spots.

Ossicones: two main ossicones. Males have one prominent median ossicone.

Population in 1960s: 1,330
Population in 2016: 1,671
Status: Increasing
Red List status: Near Threatened
Population in zoos worldwide: 450

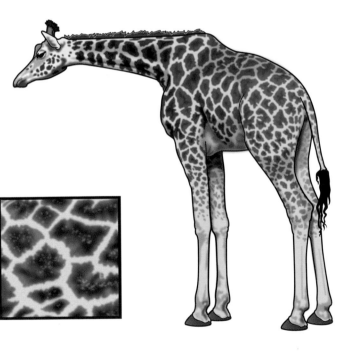

Subspecies: Thornicroft's giraffe *(G. c. thornicrofti)*
Where they are found: Luangwa Valley of Zambia

Coat color and pattern: irregularly shaped. Some are star-shaped. The spots are not as dark as those of the Masai giraffe. The spots on the neck are larger, and the legs may or may not have spots.

Ossicones: two main ossicones. Males have one median ossicone that is small and less obvious than the other two.

Population in 1980s: 600
Population in 2016: 600
Status: Stable
Red List status: Vulnerable
Population in zoos worldwide: 0

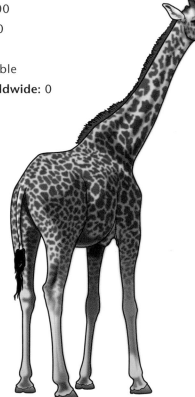

REGION: SOUTHERN AFRICA

Several giraffe populations in sections of Botswana, Zimbabwe, Namibia, and Zambia could be either Angolan or South African giraffes. The IUCN combines them as Angolan.

Subspecies: Angolan giraffe *(G. c. angolensis)*
Where they are found: savannas of Namibia and Botswana. Some have been translocated to Zimbabwe and South Africa.

Coat color and pattern: large and brown with notched edges. On the legs and backside, the spots are smaller and continue down the legs. Each ear has a white patch.

Ossicones: Males and females each have two main ossicones. Males do not have a prominent median ossicone.

Population in 1980s: 5,000
Population in 2016: 13,031
Status: Increasing
Red List status: Least Concern
Population in zoos worldwide: 20

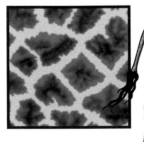

Subspecies: South African giraffe *(G. c. giraffa)*

Where they are found: savannas of South Africa, Zimbabwe, Mozambique, and Botswana

Coat color and pattern: The background color of this giraffe is tannish, darker than the color of other subspecies. The spots are brown and smaller as they go farther down the legs.

Ossicones: Males and females have two main ossicones. Males do not have a prominent median ossicone.

Population in 1970s: 8,000
Population in 2016: 21,387
Status: Increasing
Red List status: Vulnerable
Population in zoos worldwide: 45

GLOSSARY

acacia: a tree or shrub of warm climates that bears spikes or clusters of yellow or white flowers and is frequently thorny. It is a preferred food of the giraffe.

albinism: an inherited absence of pigment in the skin and hair (which are white) and the eyes (which are usually pink)

anatomy: the branch of science that studies the body structure of humans, animals, and other living organisms

anthrax: a bacterial disease, typically affecting the skin and lungs. Anthrax affects sheep and cattle in Africa.

Big Five: the five most sought-after trophy animals in game hunting—the African lion, African elephant, African leopard, African white or black rhino, and African buffalo

binomial system: a formal system of naming and classifying living things by giving each a name composed of two parts, the first for the genus and the second for the species. Carl Linnaeus developed the system in the eighteenth century.

biodiversity: the variety of life in the world or in a particular habitat or ecosystem

botanist: an expert in or student of the scientific study of plants

bushmeat: the meat of African wild animals. People often eat or sell the meat.

catalog: to make a systematic list of items of the same type

conservation: prevention of wasteful use of a resource

conservation status: the ranking of a species according to its risk of global extinction

corridor: a long passage from one area to another. Animals travel along natural corridors to move to areas where they will find mates, food, and other necessities of life.

deforestation: clearing a wide area of trees, usually for homes, ranches, or other human activities

delist: to remove from a list or category

desertification: the process by which fertile land becomes desert, typically as a result of drought, deforestation, or types of agriculture unsuitable for the area

ecosystem: a biological community of organisms and the physical environment in which they live

estrus: a recurring period of sexual receptivity and fertility in many female mammals. Also known as heat.

evolution: the process by which different kinds of living organisms developed and diversified from earlier forms during the history of Earth. English naturalist Charles Darwin developed the theory in the early nineteenth century. He based it on the concept of natural selection, in which animals with features most well suited to their environment are the ones most likely to survive, reproduce, and pass their traits to the next generation.

field research: the collection of raw data in a subject's natural environment rather than from experiments in a laboratory or books in a library

flora: the plants of a particular region, habitat, or geological period

forage: to search widely for food

game sanctuary: a geographic area where species are protected from hunting, predators, and competition for resources

genetic diversity: the differences in genes among individuals within a species and from one species to another

gestation: carrying or being carried in the womb between conception and birth; also known as pregnancy

giraffid: a member of the giraffe family of mammals. These animals include giraffes and okapi.

Great Migration: the largest round-trip land migration of animals in the world, primarily wildebeests, zebras, and Thomson's gazelles, occurring during the annual dry season (between June and October) and moving from Tanzania to Kenya in eastern Africa and back again. The animals are looking for food and water.

habitat: the natural home or environment of an animal, plant, or organism

hock: the joint in an animal's hind leg between the knee and the hoof area, comparable to the ankle in a human

hybrid: the offspring of two plants or animals of different species or subspecies, such as a mule (a hybrid of a donkey and a horse); also known as a crossbreed

infrasonic: sound waves with a frequency below the lower limit of a human's ability to hear

infrastructure: the basic physical and organizational buildings, roads, and other facilities that help a society or enterprise function

keystone species: a species on which other species in an ecosystem largely depend. If a keystone species dies off or is removed, the ecosystem will change drastically.

leucism: a genetic condition in which a plant or animal has a partial loss of pigmentation (color)

megafauna: the largest mammals of a particular region, habitat, or geological period

ossicone: a hornlike or antler-like knob on the head of a giraffe and male okapi. Giraffids have at least two ossicones.

osteophagia: licking, eating, or chewing bones of animals for the calcium, potassium, and other nutrients they contain

parasitic: a type of biological relationship in which one organism lives on or in another organism, known as the host, to benefit from that organism's nutrients, to reproduce, to raise their young, and to carry out other aspects of the life cycle. The relationship causes some harm to the host and sometimes death.

physiology: the branch of biology that studies the functions of living organisms and their body parts

pica: a craving to eat substances other than those an animal typically relies on for food

poaching: illegal hunting

predation: preying on animals for food. Predation is part of the life cycle of most animals on Earth.

prehensile: capable of grasping. Animals, including humans, have appendages such as tails, limbs, fingers, and toes that can grasp a wide range of items to help them eat, hunt, mate, travel, and express affection.

reticulated: constructed, arranged, or marked like a net or a network. Some giraffes have reticulated spotting on their coats.

rinderpest: sometimes called cattle plague, this infectious viral disease impacts cattle and other ruminants (cud-chewing animals)

safari: an expedition to observe or hunt animals in the wild in their natural habitat in Africa

savanna: a grassy plain with few trees in tropical and subtropical regions of the world

snare: a trap for catching birds and other animals, typically including a noose made of wire or cord

species: a taxonomic group of living organisms in which individuals share many traits and can actually or potentially interbreed in nature

subsistence farming: raising crops, livestock, or both to provide all or almost all the goods a family needs to survive, usually without extra for sale to others

subspecies: a taxonomic category of living organisms that share a high percentage of traits. Unlike a species, which can live in various places around the globe, subspecies usually live in geographic isolation from the species.

symbiotic: a relationship between two organisms that live in close physical contact. The relationship usually benefits both life-forms in some way.

taxonomy: the science of identifying, naming, and classifying organisms

translocation: moving something from one place to another

trophy hunting: killing wild animals for their body parts, such as the head, tusks, antlers, and hide, for display and not primarily for food

ungulate: a hoofed mammal

zoologist: an expert in or student of the behavior, physiology, classification, and distribution of animals

SOURCE NOTES

4 Isak Dinesen, *Out of Africa and Shadows on the Grass* (New York: Vintage International, 1938), 22.

7 Sarah Knapton, "Sir David Attenborough: Giraffe Are Facing 'Silent Extinction,'" *Telegraph* (London), June 18, 2016, https://www.telegraph .co.uk/science/2016/06/18/sir-david-attenborough-giraffes-are-facing -silent-extinction/.

7 Knapton.

8 Damian Carrington, "Giraffe Facing Extinction after Devastating Decline, Experts Warn," *Guardian* (US edition), December 8, 2016, https://www.theguardian.com/environment/2016/dec/08/giraffe-red-list -vulnerable-species-extinction.

8 "About," IUCN, accessed December 4, 2018, https://www.iucn.org/about.

11 Carrington, "Giraffe."

12 Anne Innis Dagg, *Pursuing Giraffe: A 1950s Adventure* (Waterloo, ONT: Wilfrid Laurier University Press, 2006), 18.

12 Dagg, 22.

15 Dagg, 57.

30 Adam Vaughan, "Giraffes Fitted with GPS Collars in Pioneering Conservation Project," *Guardian* (US edition), February 15, 2010, https:// www.theguardian.com/environment/2010/feb/15/giraffes-gps-collars -conservation.

31 Stephanie Fennessy, email to author, January 22, 2018.

39 Karl Gruber, "Giraffes Spend Their Evenings Humming to Each Other," *New Scientist,* September 17, 2015, https://www.newscientist.com/article /2058123-giraffes-spend-their-evenings-humming-to-each-other/.

40 Barry Yeoman, "When Animals Grieve," National Wildlife Foundation, January 30, 2018, https://www.nwf.org/Home/Magazines/National -Wildlife/2018/Feb-Mar/Animals/When-Animals-Grieve.

41 Yeoman.

42 Yeoman.

44 Adam Vaughan, "Researchers Discover There Are Not One—but Four Species of Giraffe," *Guardian* (US edition), September 8, 2016, https:// www.theguardian.com/environment/2016/sep/08/researchers-discover -there-are-not-one-but-four-species-of-giraffe.

44 Vaughan.

45 Anne Innis Dagg, *Giraffe Biology, Behavior and Conservation* (New York: Cambridge University Press, 2014), 25.

45 Zoe Muller, email to author, February 23, 2018.

51 Jules Howard, "We Are to Blame for the Decline of Giraffes. And Only We Can Save Them," *Guardian* (US edition), December 8, 2016, https://www.theguardian.com/global/commentisfree/2016/dec/08/giraffes-decline-vulnerable-species.

55 Joshua Rapp Learn, "Birds Sleep in Giraffe Armpits, New Photos Reveal," *National Geographic,* February 27, 2018, https://news.nationalgeographic.com/2018/02/animals-serengeti-tanzania-birds/.

57 Scott Ramsay, "Africa's Oldest Wilderness under Threat from Mining," *Africa Geographic,* June 12, 2014, https://africageographic.com/blog/africas-oldest-wilderness-under-threat-from-mining/.

57 Ramsay.

58 Yonette Joseph, "Rare White Giraffes Cause a Stir in Kenya," *New York Times,* September 16, 2017, https://www.nytimes.com/2017/09/16/world/africa/rare-white-giraffe-kenya.html.

59 Bryan Shorrocks, *The Giraffe: Biology, Ecology, Evolution and Behavior* (Chichester, West Sussex, UK: John Wiley & Sons, 2016), 178.

62–63 Tiffany Misrahi, "Together Let's Stop the $23 Billion Illegal Wildlife Industry," Medium.com, October 11, 2018, https://medium.com/@WTTC/together-lets-stop-the-23-billion-illegal-wildlife-industry-32e11bd61b07.

64 Henry Austin, "Giraffes in Danger of Extinction: Numbers Plummet by 40 Per Cent in Just 15 Years Thanks to Poachers after Their Meat and Bone Marrow," *Daily Mail.com,* December 3, 2014, http://www.dailymail.co.uk/news/article-2858734/Giraffes-danger-extinction-Numbers-plummet-40-cent-just-15-years-thanks-poachers.html.

64 Henry Austin, "Giraffes Suffocated in Wire Traps," *Daily Mail.com,* December 9, 2014, http://www.dailymail.co.uk/news/article-2865097/The-cruel-trade-Giraffe-meat-sees-trapped-vicious-snares-hacked-death-machetes-sold-little-30p-pound.html#ixzz59pTjwRqX.

64 Austin.

64–65 Austin.

66 John R. Platt, "Poachers Are Now Slaughtering Africa's Giraffes," TakePart, November 20, 2014, http://www.takepart.com/article/2014/11/19/giraffes-are-poachers-newest-target.

70   "ESA Basics: 40 Years of Conserving Endangered Species," US Fish and
     Wildlife Service, January 2013, https://www.fws.gov/endangered/esa
     -library/pdf/ESA_basics.pdf.

74   Bjorn Carey, "Sahara Desert Was Once Lush and Populated," Live Science
     Online, July 20, 2006, https://www.livescience.com/4180-sahara-desert
     -lush-populated.html.

77   Oliver Milman, "Conservationists Say Giraffes Are at Risk of 'Silent
     Extinction," Business Insider, April 19, 2017, http://www.businessinsider
     .com/giraffes-are-at-risk-of-silent-extinction-2017-4.

86   *Last of the Longnecks (Walking with Giraffes),* DVD, directed by Ashley
     Scott Davison (New Braunfels, TX: Iniosante Studios, 2017).

88   Zoe Muller, "Sticking Their Necks Out," *Africa Geographic,* August 2011,
     16.

88–89 Muller, 17.

89   "Operation Twiga II—Saving Uganda's Threatened Nubian Giraffe,"
     Giraffe Conservation Foundation, September 1, 2017, https://
     giraffeconservation.org/2017/09/01/operation-twiga-2/.

93   "Snares to Wares," MSU Today, accessed January 5, 2019, https://
     msutoday.msu.edu/feature/2016/snares-to-wares/.

93   "Snares to Wares."

SELECTED BIBLIOGRAPHY

Actman, Jani. "Giraffes Are Being Killed for Their Tails." *National Geographic,* August 10, 2016. https://news.nationalgeographic.com/2016/08/wildlife-giraffes -garamba-national-park-poaching-tails/.

Austin, Henry. "Giraffes in Danger of Extinction: Numbers Plummet by 40 Per Cent in Just 15 Years Thanks to Poachers after Their Meat and Bone Marrow." *Daily Mail.com.* December 3, 2014. http://www.dailymail.co.uk/news/article -2858734/Giraffes-danger-extinction-Numbers-plummet-40-cent-just-15-years -thanks-poachers.html.

———. "Giraffes Suffocated in Wire Traps." *Daily Mail.com,* December 9, 2014. http://www.dailymail.co.uk/news/article-2865097/The-cruel-trade-Giraffe-meat -sees-trapped-vicious-snares-hacked-death-machetes-sold-little-30p-pound .html#ixzz59pTjwRqX.

Ben Khatra, Nabil, and Maud Loireau. "The Immense Challenge of Desertification in Sub-Saharan Africa." Phys.org, October 5, 2017. https://phys .org/news/2017-10-immense-desertification-insub-saharan-africa.html.

Bercovitch, Fred, Philip S. M. Berry, Anne Dagg, Francois Deacon, John B. Doherty, Derek Lee, Frédéric Mineur, Zoe Muller, Rob Ogden, Russell Seymour, Bryan Shorrocks, and Andy Tutchings. "How Many Species of Giraffe Are There?" *Current Biology* 27, no. 4, February 20, 2017, R136–137.

Boissoneault, Lorraine. "What Really Turned the Sahara Desert from a Green Oasis into a Wasteland?" *Smithsonian.com,* March 24, 2017. https://www .smithsonianmag.com/science-nature/what-really-turned-sahara-desert-green -oasis-wasteland-180962668.

Brogan, Jacob. "How a Tiny Worm Is Irritating the Most Majestic of Giraffes." *Smithsonian.com,* May 19, 2017. https://www.smithsonianmag.com/smithsonian -institution/how-tiny-worm-is-irritating-most-majestic-giraffes-180963260/.

Carey, Bjorn. "Sahara Desert Was Once Lush and Populated." Live Science Online, July 20, 2006. https://www.livescience.com/4180-sahara-desert-lush -populated.html.

Carrington, Damian. "Giraffes Facing Extinction after Devastating Decline, Experts Warn." *Guardian* (US edition), December 8, 2016. https://www .theguardian.com/environment/2016/dec/08/giraffe-red-list-vulnerable-species -extinction.

Cheever, Frederico, and Annecoos Wiersma. "Giraffes Are in Trouble—the U.S. Endangered Species Act Can Help." Conversation, May 17, 2017. http:// theconversation.com/giraffes-are-in-trouble-the-us-endangered-species-act-can -help-77380.

Dagg, Anne Innis. *5 Giraffes.* Markham, ONT: Fitzhenry & Whiteside, 2016.

———. *Giraffe Biology, Behavior and Conservation.* New York: Cambridge University Press, 2014.

———. *A Personal History of Anne Innis Dagg as Zoologist.* Accessed January 28, 2018. http://annedagg.net/docs/webzoolhist.pdf#zoom=85.

———. *Pursuing Giraffe: A 1950s Adventure.* Waterloo, ONT: Wilfrid Laurier University Press, 2006.

"Delisted Species." US Fish and Wildlife Service, December 18, 2018. https://ecos.fws.gov/ecp0/reports/delisting-report.

"ESA Basics: 40 Years of Conserving Endangered Species." US Fish and Wildlife Service, January 2013. https://www.fws.gov/endangered/esa-library/pdf/ESA_basics.pdf.

Fennessy, Julian, Stephanie Fennessy, and A. Muneza. *Africa-Wide Giraffe Conservation Strategic Framework: Road Map.* Windhoek, Namibia: Giraffe Conservation Foundation, 2016.

"GCF Conservation Status." Giraffe Conservation Foundation. Accessed January 6, 2019. https://giraffeconservation.org/programmes/giraffe-conservation-status/.

Gibbens, Sarah. "Giraffes Seen Feasting on Skeletons—Here's Why." *National Geographic,* July 6, 2017. https://news.nationalgeographic.com/2017/07/giraffes-eat-skeletons-bones-spd/.

Giraffe Conservation Foundation. *Africa's Giraffe (*Giraffa camelopardalis*): A Conservation Guide.* Black Eagle Media: Western Cape, South Africa, 2016. https://giraffeconservation.org/wp-content/uploads/2016/03/Africas-Giraffe-A-conservation-guide.pdf.

"GPS Tracking Being Used on Giraffe for Species Conservation." LiveViewGPS, July 26, 2017. https://www.liveviewgps.com/blog/gps-tracking-giraffe-species-conservation/.

Hamlin, David. "These Rare Giraffes Were Killed Just for Their Tails." *National Geographic,* August 10, 2016. https://video.nationalgeographic.com/video/news/00000156-7491-dca8-ab77-7dd94ec40000?source=searchvideo. 8.5 min.

Hayward, Matt. "Giraffes Aren't Dangerous—but They Will Soon Be Endangered." Phys.org, August 7, 2015. https://phys.org/news/2015-08-giraffes-dangerous-beendangered.html.

Howard, Jules. "We Are to Blame for the Decline of Giraffes. And Only We Can Save Them." *Guardian* (US edition), December 8, 2016. https://www.theguardian.com/global/commentisfree/2016/dec/08/giraffes-decline-vulnerable-species.

Humane Society of the United States and Humane Society International. *Trophy Hunting by the Numbers: The United States' Role in Global Trophy Hunting.* February 2016. http://www.hsi.org/assets/pdfs/report_trophy_hunting_by_the.pdf.

———. "Undercover Investigation Exposes Shocking, Unregulated Market for Giraffe Parts across the United States Despite Steep Population Declines," news release, August 23, 2018. https://www.humanesociety.org/news/undercover -investigation-exposes-shocking-unregulated-market-giraffe-parts-across-united.

IUCN. *IUCN Red List Categories and Criteria: Version 3.1.* 2nd ed. Gland, Switzerland: IUCN, 2012.

IUCN Species Survival Commission's Species Conservation Planning Sub-Committee. *Guidelines for Species Conservation Planning.* Version 1.0. Gland, Switzerland: IUCN, 2017.

Joseph, Yonette. "Rare White Giraffes Cause a Stir in Kenya." *New York Times,* September 16, 2017. https://www.nytimes.com/2017/09/16/world/africa/rare -white-giraffe-kenya.html.

Knapton, Sarah. "Sir David Attenborough: Giraffes Are Facing 'Silent Extinction.'" *Telegraph* (London), June 18, 2016. https://www.telegraph.co.uk/ science/2016/06/18/sir-david-attenborough-giraffes-are-facing-silent-extinction/.

Lagueux, Olivier. "Geoffroy's Giraffe: The Hagiography of a Charismatic Mammal." *Journal of the History of Biology* 36, no. 2. (Summer 2003): 225–247. https://www.jstor.org/stable/4331801.

Learn, Joshua Rapp. "Birds Sleep in Giraffe Armpits, New Photos Reveal." *National Geographic,* February 27, 2018. https://news.nationalgeographic.com /2018/02/animals-serengeti-tanzania-birds/.

"Listing Species under the Endangered Species Act." Convention on Biological Diversity. Accessed January 3, 2019. https://www.biologicaldiversity.org/programs /biodiversity/endangered_species_act/listing_species_under_the_endangered _species_act/index.html.

Maisano, Sarah. "*Giraffa camelopardalis* Giraffe." Animal Diversity Web. Accessed February 08, 2018. http://animaldiversity.org/accounts/Giraffa_camclopardalis/.

Margulis, Jennifer. "Things Are Looking Up for Niger's Wild Giraffes." *Smithsonian,* November 2008. https://www.smithsonianmag.com/science-nature /things-are-looking-up-for-nigers-wild-giraffes-83484347/#hqfTVPpjs CUmqFBD.99.

Milman, Oliver. "Conservationists Say Giraffes Are at Risk of 'Silent Extinction.'" Business Insider, April 19, 2017. https://www.businessinsider.com/giraffes-are-at -risk-of-silent-extinction-2017-4.

Misrahi, Tiffany. "Together Let's Stop the $23 Billion Illegal Wildlife Industry." Medium.com, October 11, 2018. https://medium.com/@WTTC/together-lets-stop-the-23-billion-illegal-wildlife-industry-32e11bd61b07.

Muller, Zoe. "The Curious Incident of the Giraffe in the Night Time." *Giraffa* 4, no. 1 (December 2010): 20–23.

———. "Population Structure of Giraffes Is Affected by Management in the Great Rift Valley, Kenya." *PLoS One.* January 3, 2018. https://journals.plos.org/plosone/article?id=10.1371/journal.pone.0189678.

————. "Sticking Their Necks Out." *Africa Geographic,* August 2011, n.p.

"One Family's Journey to Save Giraffe." WildArk. Accessed January 2, 2019. https://wildark.com/blog/one-familys-journey-save-giraffe/.

"Operation Twiga Field Report: Murchison Falls National Park, Uganda, January 2016." Giraffe Conservation Foundation. https://giraffeconservation.org/wp-content/uploads/2016/02/Operation-Twiga-Report-January-2016.pdf.

Panko, Ben. "How Do Giraffes Stay So Cool? Perhaps the Secret Is a Long Neck." *Smithsonian.com,* September 14, 2017. https://www.smithsonianmag.com/smart-news/how-do-giraffes-stay-so-cool-those-necks-180964890/.

Parham, Donna. "Wildwatch Kenya: Help Wanted." San Diego Zoo Global Zoonooz, June 19, 2017. https://zoonooz.sandiegozoo.org/2017/06/19/wildwatch-kenya-help-wanted/.

Platt, John R. "Conservationists Rush to Save the Congo's Last 38 Giraffes." TakePart, February 2, 2016. http://www.takepart.com/article/2016/02/02/conservationists-rush-save-congos-last-38-giraffes.

———. "Poachers Are Now Slaughtering Africa's Giraffes." TakePart, November 20, 2014. http://www.takepart.com/article/2014/11/19/giraffes-are-poachers-newest-target.

Princeton University. "The Ecological Costs of War: Conflict a Consistent Killer of African Megafauna." ScienceDaily, January 10, 2018. https://www.sciencedaily.com/releases/2018/01/180110131516.htm.

Ramsay, Scott. "Africa's Oldest Wilderness under Threat from Mining." *Africa Geographic,* June 12, 2014. https://africageographic.com/blog/africas-oldest-wilderness-under-threat-from-mining/.

Rice, Xan. "Giraffe Numbers in Masai Mara Down 95%." *Guardian* (US edition), April 21, 2009. https://www.theguardian.com/environment/2009/apr/22/kenya-giraffes-maasai.

"Saving the Last West African Giraffe." Sahara Conservation Fund. Accessed March 20, 2018. https://www.saharaconservation.org/Saving_West_African_Giraffe.

Shorrocks, Bryan. *The Giraffe: Biology, Ecology, Evolution, and Behavior.* Chichester, West Sussex, UK: John Wiley & Sons, 2016.

Smith, Phillip. "The Lone Drone on a Mission to Save Rare Nigerian White Giraffes." DroneBelow, March 2, 2018. https://dronebelow.com/2018/03/02/lone -drone-mission-save-rare-nigerian-white-giraffes/.

Smuts, Rowena. *Are Partnerships the Key to Conserving Africa's Biodiversity? Four Partnership Case Studies between Mining Companies and Conservation NGOs.* Arlington, VA: Conservation International, 2010.

"Snares to Wares." MSU Today. Accessed January 5, 2019. https://msutoday.msu .edu/feature/2016/snares-to-wares/.

"UNESCO Expresses Concern over the State of Conservation of Selous Game Reserve (United Republic of Tanzania)." UNESCO, February 22, 2018. http:// whc.unesco.org/en/news/1785/.

Vaughan, Adam. "Giraffes Fitted with GPS Collars in Pioneering Conservation Project." *Guardian* (US edition), February 15, 2010. https://www.theguardian.com /environment/2010/feb/15/giraffes-gps-collars-conservation.

———. "Researchers Discover There Are Not One—but Four Species of Giraffe." *Guardian* (US edition), September 8, 2016. https://www.theguardian.com /environment/2016/sep/08/researchers-discover-there-are-not-one-but-four-species -of-giraffe.

Weisberger, Mindy. "The Sahara Desert Is Growing and Here's What That Means." Live Science, March 29, 2018. https://www.livescience.com/62168 -sahara-desert-expanding.html.

"Why Is Taxonomy Important?" Convention of Biological Diversity. Accessed January 6, 2019. https://www.cbd.int/gti/importance.shtml.

"The World's Largest Rock Art Petroglyph: Giraffe Carvings of the Sahara Desert." Bradshaw Foundation. Accessed January 5, 2019. http://www .bradshawfoundation.com/giraffe/artists.php.

Yeoman, Barry. "When Animals Grieve." National Wildlife Federation, January 30, 2018. https://www.nwf.org/Home/Magazines/National-Wildlife/2018/Feb -Mar/Animals/When-Animals-Grieve.

FURTHER INFORMATION

Books

Dagg, Anne Innis. *Smitten by Giraffe: My Life as a Citizen Scientist.* Montreal: McGill-Queen's University Press, 2016.

Downer, Ann. *The Animal Mating Game: The Wacky, Weird World of Sex in the Animal Kingdom.* Minneapolis: Twenty-First Century Books, 2017.

Fleischman, Paul. *Eyes Wide Open: Going beyond the Environmental Headlines.* Somerville, MA: Candlewick Press, 2014.

Gelletly, LeeAnne. *Ecological Issues: Africa: Progress & Problems.* Broomall, PA: Mason Crest, 2006.

Hirsch, Rebecca E. *De-extinction: The Science of Bringing Lost Species Back to Life.* Minneapolis: Twenty-First Century Books, 2017.

McPherson, Stephanie Sammartino. *Arctic Thaw: Climate Change and the Global Race for Energy Resources.* Minneapolis: Twenty-First Century Books, 2015.

Nustad, Knut. *Creating Africas: Struggles over Nation, Conservation and Land.* London: C. Hurst, 2015.

Peterson, Dale, and Karl Ammann. *Giraffe Reflections.* Berkeley, CA: University of California Press, 2013.

Sherr, Lynn. *Tall Blondes: A Book about Giraffes.* Kansas City, MO: Andrews McMeel, 1997.

Documentaries

Giraffes: Africa's Gentle Giants, AGB Films and BBC, televised on *Nature*/PBS, 2016. 53 min.
In collaboration with a determined Ugandan Wildlife Authority team, Julian Fennessy, cofounder of the Giraffe Conservation Foundation, works with a trained team to move some of the world's rarest giraffes to a new area where they can safely live and reproduce. To do this, they must find a way to carefully ferry these gentle giants across the mighty Nile River.

Last of the Longnecks (Walking with Giraffes), NatGeo. New Braunfels, TX: Iniosante Studios. http://www.lastofthelongnecks.com. 92 min.
Planned as a series of conservation films, NatGeo follows scientists and conservationists to show and tell the story of the decline of giraffes in the wild and the consequences of their possible extinction. Episode I, "Walking with Giraffes" premiered on Nat Geo WILD in May 2017. Two more episodes—"Catching Giants" and "Saving a Species"—will eventually air on PBS.

Websites

African Wildlife Foundation
https://www.awf.org
This organization's website provides a wide array of information on the flora, fauna, and conservation needs and efforts across Africa.

Anne Innis Dagg
http://www.annedagg.net
Dagg's personal website provides information about her studies, publications, and work as a zoologist and feminist. The related website www.thewomanwholoves giraffes.com includes a trailer for a new film about her life.

Care for Karamoja
http://www.care4karamoja.org
This site provides a look into the people and animals, especially Rothschild's giraffes and ostriches, in the Karamoja area of northeastern Uganda. It includes a five-minute video about the work the project is doing.

Giraffe Conservation Alliance (GCA)
http://www.giraffealliance.org
The website describes the program's mission to connect people and zoos around the world with giraffe conservation projects in Africa. Videos and giraffe facts are available.

Giraffe Conservation Foundation (GCF)
https://www.giraffeconservation.org
This is by far the most comprehensive website about giraffes on the internet. Viewers will find the most up-to-date information, infographics, maps, downloadable reports, Operation Twiga updates, and much more. Opportunities to support the foundation on the website include Adopt a Giraffe, and information on World Giraffe Day. You can sign up to receive their newsletter too.

Giraffe Resource Centre
https://www.girafferesourcecentre.org
Sponsored by the Giraffe Conservation Foundation, this website houses a database of more than three hundred reports and articles about giraffes, which are downloadable as pdfs. Its goal is to collect, preserve, and make available materials about giraffes in one accessible location.

IUCN SSC Giraffe and Okapi Specialist Group
http://www.giraffidsg.org
The official website for the IUCN Species Survival Commission Giraffe and Okapi Specialist Group provides information about giraffes, okapis, and the latest news on those species. Key resources about okapi are available on this website. Information about giraffes is found via a link to a new comprehensive resource center at www.girafferesourcecentre.org.

Jeans for Giraffes
http://www.jeansforgiraffes.org
The Jeans for Giraffes project raises money for giraffe conservation through collecting and recycling denim from donated jeans. The programs they support and donation locations are listed on the website.

Project GIRAFFE, Tanzania
https://www.wildnatureinstitute.org/giraffe.html
The Wild Nature Institute conducts scientific research on several at-risk species, including the giraffe. You can find out about Project GIRAFFE, which studies the effects of human and natural activities on the habitat of Masai giraffes. Money raised via the website comes from three options: direct donations, sales of the children's book *Juma the Giraffe,* and the Adopt-a-Giraffe program.

Reticulated Giraffe Project, Kenya
http://www.reticulatedgiraffeproject.net
Videos, photos, articles, and information about the conservation efforts for the reticulated giraffes of Kenya make up the pages of this website. The site provides a long and impressive list of partners, including Anne Innis Dagg and dozens of zoos around the world. Donations may be made on the site.

Rothschild's Giraffe Project, Kenya and Uganda
http://www.girafferesearch.com
Information specific to the Rothschild's giraffe and the Rothschild's Giraffe Project's research and projects are displayed on the website. The media page offers pdfs, articles, photos, and other resources about giraffe conservation.

Snares to Wares, Uganda
https://www.recaplaboratory.com/snares-to-wares.html
Michigan State University's conservation program, Research on the Ecology of Carnivores and their Prey, created this website to inform viewers about their work on behalf of wildlife conservation. You can learn about the Snares to Wares project here.

Wildwatch Kenya
https://www.zooniverse.org/projects/sandiegozooglobal/wildwatch-kenya
This citizen-science project website is where volunteers can sign up to help with the Wildwatch Kenya project. More than thirteen thousand volunteers have already logged in, and they count, identify, and track giraffes in northern Kenya.

Zooniverse
http://www.zooniverse.com
The world's largest people-powered research platform offers ordinary citizens opportunities to get involved in a wide variety of research studies—from science to history to literature and more.

INDEX

acacia trees
   and giraffes, 7, 50
   as source of water, 73, 76
activism, 70–71

Big Five, 56, 67–68
bushmeat, 62, 64–65, 91

Carson, Rachel, 70
citizen science, 94–96
   Wildwatch Kenya, 96
   Zooniverse, 96
conservation groups, 9, 81, 91, 95–97
   African Parks Network, 67
   African Wildlife Foundation, 84
   Association for Saving the Giraffes of
      Niger, 82–83
   Center for Biological Diversity, 71
   Giraffe Conservation Foundation, 7, 11,
      18, 28, 30–31, 43–47, 72, 80–82, 84,
      87–89, 98
   International Fund for Animal Welfare,
      71, 77
   International Union for Conservation
      of Nature (IUCN), 7–11, 18, 28, 44,
      59, 82
   Kissama Foundation, 62
   Species Survival Commission Giraffe
      and Okapi Specialist Group, 18, 23,
      26, 80–81
   Wild Nature Institute, 91
conservationists, 10–11, 15–16, 19, 25, 28,
      30–31, 45, 70, 78–79
   Abdullahi H. Ali, 58
   Inger Andersen, 8
   John Doherty, 85–86
   Julian Fennessy, 11, 26, 30, 43–44, 66,
      79–81
   Stephanie Fennessy, 31, 79–80
   Zoe Muller, 17, 40–41, 45, 87–89
conservation projects, 71, 80–82, 84,
      92–93, 96
   Adopt a Giraffe, 80
   BOMA Project, 86
   Operation Noah's Ark, 62
   Operation Twiga, 89–90

Project GIRAFFE, 90–91
   Reticulated Giraffe Project, 85–86
   Rothschild's Giraffe Project, 86–89
   Snares to Wares, 91–93
   World Giraffe Day, 89–90, 97–98
Convention on International Trade in
      Endangered Species of Wild Fauna
      and Flora (CITES), 70
   and giraffes, 72
   infographic, 46

deforestation, 50, 59, 71
desertification, 76
   infographic, 75
   Sahara shift, 74–75
drought, 28, 49, 67, 71–76, 82, 91

ecosystems, 6–7, 9–10, 52, 54, 59, 70, 78
endangered species, 47, 62, 65, 69
Endangered Species Act, 69–70
   and giraffes, 71
estrus
   and giraffes, 35–36
   hormone, 36
extinction, 25–26, 51, 56, 59, 70, 72, 79,
      86
   and giraffes, 5, 7, 11, 16, 19, 61–62,
      93, 97
   infographic, 9
   and IUCN Red List, 8–10, 44–47, 82

fund-raising, 97–99

giraffe behavior, 4–5, 14–15, 28, 32–33, 82
   communication, 38–39
   diet, 7, 28, 33, 35, 73, 76
   grieving, 40–42
   mating (*see* necking)
   osteophagia, 42
   reproduction, 17, 33, 36, 43
   symbiosis (*see* yellow-billed oxpeckers)
giraffe biology, 32, 39
   body temperature, 36–38
   evolution of, 11, 34–36, 38
   heart, 29–30
   hide patterns, 21, 23, 27, 31, 38, 44
   hooves, 27, 34, 90

neck, 11, 34–39
ossicones, 21, 27, 29–31
giraffe habitat, 19–20, 28, 30–31, 38,
    48–53, 55, 59, 64–68, 82–83, 88, 91
    infographic, 100
giraffe parts, uses of, 64–66
    decoration, 65–66
    food (*See* bushmeat)
    jewelry, 65–66
    medicine, 65
    and poaching, 64–66
Giraffes: Africa's Gentle Giants, 18–19
giraffe subspecies, 11, 14, 18–19, 23, 25,
    27–28, 42–47, 82, 86–87, 96
    Angolan giraffe (*Giraffa angolensis*), 25,
        44, 46, 62
    Kordofan giraffe (*Giraffa camelopardalis
        antiquorum*), 25, 44, 46, 65, 67
    Masai giraffe (*Giraffa camelopardalis
        tippelskirchi*), 25, 44, 46–47, 52–53,
        90–91
    Nubian giraffe (*Giraffa camelopardalis
        camelopardalis*), 25, 44, 46
    reticulated giraffe (*Giraffa camelopardalis
        reticulata*), 5, 23, 25, 29, 44, 46–47,
        52–53, 58, 85–86
    Rothschild's giraffe (*Giraffa
        camelopardalis rothschildi*), 16, 18–19,
        25, 52–53, 86–90
    South African giraffe (*Giraffa
        camelopardalis giraffa*), 25, 44, 46,
        56–57, 62
    southern giraffe (*Giraffa giraffa*), 44
    Thornicroft's giraffe (*Giraffa
        camelopardalis thornicrofti*), 25
    West African giraffe (*Giraffa
        camelopardalis peralta*), 16–18, 25, 44,
        46, 61, 82–85
governments, 13, 62, 98
    and conservation, 18, 47, 67, 70–72,
        81–85
    and mining, 56–57, 59
    and poaching, 26, 62–63
    and tourism, 53, 69

habitat, 8, 52, 70–71, 76–77
    fragmentation, 48–53, 91
    and giraffes, 19–20, 28, 30–31, 38, 55,

59, 64–68, 82–83, 88, 100
    loss of, 10, 24, 48–50, 55–59, 64, 68,
        82, 88
herbivores, 28, 42

infographics
    extinction, 9, 46
    giraffe habitat, 100
    Sahara shift, 76
    taxonomy, 25, 44
IUCN Red List of Threatened Species,
    8–11, 16, 18, 26, 44–47, 84–85
    infographic, 9

keystone species, 6–7, 82

leucism, 58

megafauna, 6, 67, 86

necking, 13–14, 33, 35
Niger, 17, 61, 63, 81
    giraffe zone, 82–85
nongovernmental organizations, 18, 67, 70,
    80–81, 84

okapi, 18, 26

parasitism, 54–55
poaching, 16, 48, 56, 62–66, 71, 82–83
    and the Big Five, 67–68
    and giraffes, 61–66, 84, 91–93
predators, 17, 26, 41, 58, 67, 73
prey, 17

Sahara shift. *See* desertification: Sahara
    shift
savanna ecosystem, 74
    and giraffes, 59
scientists, 8, 10–11, 16, 20–28, 31, 33–35,
    39–43, 70, 74–76, 79, 87, 91
    Isabelle Ciofolo, 82
    Anne Innis Dagg, 12–15, 28, 32, 35,
        45, 85
    Dian Fossey, 13
    Jane Goodall, 12–13, 15
    Carl Linnaeus, 20–22, 24
    Richard Lydekker, 23
    Robert Montgomery, 92–93
    Meredith Palmer, 55
    Étienne Geoffroy Saint-Hilaire, 22–23

social media, 69
 and citizen science, 94–96
 and giraffe conservation, 95–96

taxonomy, 10, 20–21, 24–25
 father of (*see* Carl Linnaeus)
 giraffe, 22–23, 44–47
 infographic, 25, 44
technology, 11
 GiraffeSpotter, 31
 GPS, 28–29
 ossi-units, 29–31
 threats to giraffes, 50
 tracking devices, 28–31
translocation projects, 62, 88–90

ungulates, 15
United Nations Educational, Scientific and
 Cultural Organization (UNESCO),
 6, 59

US Fish and Wildlife Service, 69

wars, 60–61, 76, 86
 and giraffes, 28, 48, 62, 66–67
wildlife parks
 Gadabeji Game Reserve, 85
 Hluhluwe-iMfolozi Park, 56–57
 Kissama National Park, 62
 Kouré Reserve, 84
 Madikwe Game Preserve, 62
 Masai Mara National Reserve, 52–53, 91
 Murchison Falls National Park, 89,
  92–93
 Samburu National Reserve, 5, 85
 Selous Game Reserve, 59
 Serengeti National Park, 55
 Zakouma National Park, 66–67
wildlife trafficking, 62–63

yellow-billed oxpeckers, 54–55

PHOTO ACKNOWLEDGMENTS

Image credits: Design elements: abeadev/Shutterstock.com; MaryMo/
Shutterstock.com. Content: Wolfgang Kaehler/LightRocket/Getty Images,
p. 5; Westend61/Getty Images, p. 6; Laura Westlund/Independent Picture
Service, pp. 9, 25, 46, 57, 75, 100, 102–110; Independent Picture Service, p. 14;
© Christophe Courteau/NPL/Minden Pictures, p. 17; Robert HENNO/Alamy
Stock Photo, p. 19; Friedrich von Horsten/Alamy Stock Photo, p. 21; © John
Zimmermann/Minden Pictures, p. 26; © Ami Vitale/National Geographic Stock,
p. 29; Steve and Bryce Kroencke/iStockphoto/Getty Images, p. 33; PicturesWild/
Shutterstock.com, p. 34; WLDavies/Getty Images, p. 37; © Yva Momatiuk and
John Eastcott/Minden Pictures, p. 40; TONY KARUMBA/AFP/Getty Images,
p. 49; © Sean Crane/Minden Pictures, p. 53; Wolfgang Wild/EyeEm/agency/
Getty Images, p. 54; © Christophe Courteau/Minden Pictures, p. 61; Stuart
Abraham/Alamy Stock Photo, p. 68; tarabird/iStockphoto/Getty Images, p. 73;
robertharding/Alamy Stock Photo, p. 83; Charles O. Cecil/Alamy Stock Photo,
p. 84; Wolfgang Kaehler/LightRocket/Getty Images, p. 85; Courtesy of Zoe
Muller, p. 87; Lingbeek/Getty Images, p. 95.

Cover: Vicki Jauron, Babylon and Beyond/Moment RF/Getty Images.

ABOUT THE AUTHOR

Tanya Anderson is an award-winning author and editor of books for young
readers. She has written more than thirty books in children's and educational
book markets. She has also written many articles and poems for McGraw-Hill
Education. Her YA book *Tillie Pierce: Teen Eyewitness to the Battle of Gettysburg*—a
Junior Library Guild selection—is a narrative nonfiction title that was a NCSS/
CBC Notable Social Studies Trade Book for Young People and the winner of the
2014 Independent Book Publishers Association (IBPA) Benjamin Franklin Award
for Juvenile Nonfiction. Another narrative nonfiction book, *Gunpowder Girls:
The True Stories of Three Civil War Tragedies*, also won the 2017 IBPA Benjamin
Franklin Award and was a Junior Library Guild selection as well. Anderson lives
with her husband and two perfect pets in Springfield, Ohio. She spends winters in
Palm Harbor, Florida. Visit her website at www.tanyaandersonbooks.com.